DIARY
of a
SOUL

DIARY
of a
SOUL

PENNAR DAVIES

Translated by
Herbert Hughes
with an Introduction and Notes

ISBN: 978 184771 376 6

FSC

Published and printed in Wales
on paper from well maintained forests
by Y Lolfa Cyf., Talybont, Ceredigion SY24 5HE
website www.ylolfa.com
e-mail ylolfa@ylolfa.com
tel 01970 832 304
fax 832 782

CONTENTS

FOREWORD

BY THE

ARCHBISHOP OF CANTERBURY
DR ROWAN WILLIAMS

IT IS TEMPTING to wonder what sort of national reputation Pennar Davies would have enjoyed if he had not made the courageous decision to focus his creative effort on work in the Welsh language. His poetry and fiction, his acute and challenging social comment and above all his idiosyncratic and profound meditations on the Christian faith remain startlingly fresh, and it is hard to avoid the conclusion that his name would have stood in very exalted company on the national scene. But part of what Pennar had to say was that reputation is neither here nor there: what matters is integrity. And if your sense is of a calling to serve the vitality and imaginative flourishing of the Welsh-speaking community, that is what has to be done and the cost to the artistic ego is immaterial. With a mixture of magisterial calm and quiet subversiveness, Pennar Davies established himself as one of the most serious voices in the Welsh culture – specifically the Welsh Nonconformist culture – of the mid-twentieth century. If that meant being marginal to what some would have considered the great currents of British life at large, he would no doubt have said, with a smile, that the margins are normally where God is to be met in his most authentic and disturbing forms.

The fact that these meditations were first published anonymously in the weekly journal of the Welsh Union of Independents (i.e. Congregationalists) suggests that even he was aware of the need to soften a little the potential shock of a senior theologian and teacher exposing his inner life with such frankness. But when the authorship of these pieces became public (and in all honesty the disguise was never that impenetrable, whatever he may have thought!), his reputation for spiritual depth and penetration suffered not at all. Rightly so: these are pages of great beauty and real challenge. The reflections move easily from family vignettes to musings on the great classical hymns of Welsh Protestantism to observations on the European theological scene and on the bustle of international conferences.

But at the heart of everything lie two constant themes. There is the struggle to be completely honest about temptation and failure, however apparently trivial. And there is the passionate devotion to the person of Jesus, expressed in imaginative meditations on the human life of the Lord that some have found almost embarrassing in their intensity. These themes are, of course, interwoven. The genuinely overwhelming sense of the personal love of Jesus is part of what makes the gruelling self-examination possible. Jesus is both the Accuser and the Absolver – and so the diary itself is a search for both honest self-accusation and honest openness to absolution.

'What a great privilege it is to preach the Love, to preach the Cross', he writes on 15 May. Pennar's theology has been charged with doctrinal indifferentism or Pelagianism: the denial of original sin and the downplaying of divine grace – and the charge is not without some substance. Densil Morgan, in his superb and deeply sympathetic biography, cannot wholly acquit him of the 'Pelagian' accusation and observes how the deep personal devotion to Jesus can from time to time veer into sentimental fantasy. Yet the impression one has from these pages is not of someone for whom effort is more important than grace or for whom the cross of Jesus is only an *illustration* of divine compassion. And whatever his impatience with the classical credal formulations, Pennar's Christ is unmistakeably the Christ of historic Christianity, the unique vehicle of God's

7

presence and act and suffering, the divine saviour – the 'exiled King', to borrow the title of one of his best-known books which he himself took from the greatest poem of Waldo Williams.

It is an immense gift to have these meditations now made available to a wider readership through the devoted work of Herbert Hughes. We have an opportunity here to encounter one of the great Reformed Christian voices of our time: gentle, unsparing, delighting in the local and domestic, yet with a clear catholic vision. Above all, a man whose holiness is manifest in the love of God and neighbour and in unbroken longing for the full light of day, the Morning Star rising in our hearts for judgement and for mercy.

Rowan Cantuar
Lambeth Palace

The Conversion of St Paul
25 January 2011

INTRODUCTION

I AM GREATLY indebted in this introduction to the scholarly and sympathetic preface by the Rev. Dr R Tudur Jones to the second edition of this diary. He and the diarist were colleagues and friends but were theologically disparate – they have been appropriately described as the Augustine and Pelagius of Welsh theology in the twentieth century. There is certainly no question of denying the immense erudition of both. It is to Tudur Jones' credit that he could write so perceptively and critically and yet sensitively of the work.

I owe a similar debt to the Notes which he provided for the same edition. I have omitted some of these and revised others and added some of my own since a number of Welsh-language references need some explanation for English readers. Most of the Biblical quotations are from the *Good News Bible* (the Bible Societies/Harper Collins, 1982).

I have also made use of the fine Welsh biography, *Pennar Davies*, by D Densil Morgan (University of Wales Press, 2003).

*

William Thomas Davies was born on 12 November 1911 in Mountain Ash in Glamorgan. (The nom-de-plume *Pennar* was adopted by him later and this became his recognizable name.) Because of his father's serious injuries at the colliery he had to endure deprivation in his youth. He was not brought up to speak Welsh and neither was he from a 'religious' home. However, he attended a number of Sunday schools and experienced a powerful religious experience when he was twelve. But he came to look at this as a 'frenzy' owing 'more to Cybele than to Christ'. He read T H Huxley when he was seventeen and came across the word *agnostic*, a word which described his position for a time. Other influences were at work on his mind mainly from reading extensively in philosophy and literature. He also became proficient at reading and writing Welsh but it took a few years for him to gain confidence to speak it.

He graduated at Cardiff University College with first class honours in Latin in 1932, and similarly in English in 1933. He then trained as a teacher before he went to Balliol College, Oxford University, to undertake research into the life of John Bale (1495–1563) and his dramatic works, for which he gained his B.Litt. Bale was a Roman Catholic who became Protestant bishop of Ossory, and a keen sixteenth-century controversialist. Pennar received the approbation of C S Lewis and very high praise from other examiners for his work. Some of his fellow Welsh students at Oxford were to become significant figures in the nation later, like his lifetime friend Gwynfor Evans, the first Plaid Cymru M.P., and Gwilym O Williams, who later became Anglican archbishop of Wales. Following this achievement he was awarded a Commonwealth Fellowship and chose to study at Yale in America. He continued with his study of English literature and concentrated on the comedies of George Chapman (1559-1634), a poet and classicist who inspired John Keats' famous sonnet 'On first looking into Chapman's Homer'. He gained his Ph.D. for his work.

Following his stay of two years at Yale (where he was generously supported by the patronage of a mysterious lady, a Mrs Fitzgerald, who had shown the same support when he was at Balliol), he returned to Wales in 1938 where he gained a University Fellowship for two years. During this period he seems to have undergone a spiritual crisis. The nature of this crisis is unclear, although Gwynfor Evans believed that it was to do with the parlous state of Wales, both economically and culturally. Pennar insisted that it was this crisis that compelled him to turn to the Christian faith. The shadow of war was also looming and Pennar responded by registering as a conscientious objector. (Mrs Fitzgerald's patronage evaporated at this point.)

He was already composing poetry and short stories and contributing articles to various journals. He also joined the ranks of the burgeoning Anglo-Welsh literary scene. He decided to train for the ministry at Mansfield College, Oxford, where he came under the influence of Nathaniel Micklem and Cecil John Cadoux, the former a Calvinist who desired to lead Congregationalists towards a renewed classical orthodoxy and the latter, more akin to Pennar himself, a pacifist and a theological liberal. (Pennar was to write a history of the college: *Mansfield College Oxford 1886–1947* (Oxford, 1947).)

At this time he also made a purposeful and explicit commitment to Wales. He wrote: 'The war which brought me to a definite and unpopular political commitment also led me to give myself to Welsh rather than to English writing and, somewhat to my own amazement and the consternation of friends on both sides of the language fence, to the quaint life work of a "Respected" among the unspeakable Welsh people.'

He was ordained minister of the English Congregational Church at Minster Road, Cardiff in 1943 and on 26 June the same year, at Mansfield College, he was married to Rosemarie Wolff who was a nurse at Radcliffe Hospital, Oxford. There were five children of the marriage.

In 1946 he was invited to take the position of professor of church history in Bangor, north Wales, at one of the three Congregational institutions in Wales which were training men for the ministry. In 1950 he took a similar post at the Memorial College, Brecon as well as becoming deputy principal and, in 1952, the principal. In 1959 he was appointed principal of the new theological college established at Swansea when the Brecon college was united with the college which had stood in Carmarthen for over a hundred years. He retired in 1981.

He held many academic posts of importance within the University of Wales and he was awarded the degree of D.D. in 1987. He was president of the Union of Welsh Independents in

1973–74, and president of the Free Church Council of Wales in 1964–69. He was a keen supporter of Plaid Cymru and stood as its parliamentary candidate in Llanelli in 1964 and 1966.

He died on 28 December 1996.

*

There is a long and honourable tradition within Christendom of searching the secret places of the soul and of sharing confessions in writing and print for the guidance of others – ranging from the classic by Saint Augustine to John Bunyan. There are also a number of Welsh examples of confessional works and techniques, all surpassed by the work of one of the leaders of the Methodist Revival in Wales, William Williams (1717–91), called *Drws y Society Profiad* translated into English as *The Experience Meeting* Bridgend, 1973). He was also the author of numerous hymns, many of which express the inner search for God and the need for the soul to be cleansed. *Diary of a Soul* belongs to this estimable tradition.

However, we have been reminded by a number of Welsh scholars of the artistic merit of the work. It has even been described, mistakenly in my view, as a novel. It has a high literary quality and a psychological and spiritual depth that cannot be ignored. One critic writes, 'It is true that self-examination can create a sense of ennui, especially when someone is for ever accusing himself... The enterprise could, if we're honest, make someone a Pharisee in reverse: I-am-glad-that-I-am-a-sinner-in-case-I-become-too-self righteous! But for myself the fact that every one of the author's feelings are like a live electric wire creates a much more instinctive and sympathetic response than if he was analysing everything on a cerebral level alone.'[1]

*

We are reminded by Pennar's preface to his volume – which mentions the way of purification, of enlightenment and of union – of Roman Catholic mysticism, and he was to write an article, 'Yr Absen Ddwyfol' [The divine absence], which summarised the views of 97 authors on the subject – a witness to his brilliant and comprehensive scholarship.[2] His pre-eminence in this field cannot be doubted and it is difficult to fully appreciate *Diary of a Soul* without recognizing that he held the mystics in high regard. He writes: 'Despite every severe criticism, the testimony is sufficient to establish the authenticity of the mystical way and the psychological experiences which follow from its pursuance.' He further emphasized that the experiences of the mystics were the same in essence as those of ordinary worshipful believers. This arises from the common experience of those who have thought seriously of the contrast between their sinful, guilty lives and God.

For Pennar, the unity of everything is to be found in God. 'One cannot say "God is Love" in a truly meaningful way without thinking of God not only as the One but also as a relationship between One and the Other. Deep in my heart I always believed this.' This was not only an idea but an experience for him, and it is clearly reflected in *Diary of a Soul*. I sometimes wonder whether Pennar pioneered in his theology some of the questions posed by the theological turbulence which a little later gave us *Honest To God* and *Exploration into God* – both by John A T Robinson.

His spirituality was Christ-centred as reflected in this piece of autobiography: 'by concentrating my longing and need around the image I have of Jesus the Fellow man who was born under Herod the Great and who died under Pontius Pilate I encountered a change of experiences. It became impossible for me now to acquire the life-giving, challenging, contending, existential experience of 'God' without recognizing him in Jesus the carpenter, the messenger and the joyous campaigner and the broken invincible.'

His Christology was not that embraced by the creeds. These

did not sufficiently contribute to his own spirituality. He rejected the view that the gospels, in a number of sayings attributed to Jesus, quoted his actual words, believing rather that they were expressions of faith on the part of his followers. Jesus did not at any time during his ministry claim that he was the Messiah; this title evolved from the experience of the disciples after the Resurrection. 'Son of God' was not adopted by Jesus either, for this suggests that he claimed a unique relationship with his Father that others could not share. The title 'Son of Man' for him had a social not an individual significance. Following this (and other) arguments he concludes, 'I am perfectly certain that part of Jesus' glory was that he rejected all the grandiose titles that the faith of his followers and the profound respect of his worshippers have claimed for him.'

Positively he places great emphasis on knowing and experiencing Jesus, and 'recognizing his favours' (quoting Melanchthon, Luther's fellow worker). He writes, 'This saying is the key to my Christology and all my theology... But such a claim is meaningless unless it is verified in our personal experience. Being amazed by the love of broken, exalted Jesus and loving him in return... that is the experience which makes man a participant in the overwhelming joy of Thomas, that sour old unbeliever, and causes him to cry "My Lord and my God."' In *Diary of a Soul* we find that he attempts to realize Jesus through the imagination, reflecting the meditative techniques of someone like Ignatius Loyola (1491–1556), and he encourages others to take their own experiences seriously as he attempted to do in his confessions. The thoughts of Friedrich E D Schleiermacher (1768–1834), who located religion in intuition and feeling not dogma, seem to have influenced Pennar.

*

Diary of a Soul was initially published as a weekly diary (or journal) in *Y Tyst* [The witness] which is the publication of the Independents/Congregationalists in Wales. The readership would be mostly 'ordinary' church members. One wonders what their response was to some of the startling and frank confessions made by a respected principal of one of their theological colleges! The diary ran, anonymously, from 20 January 1955 until 16 February 1956, under the pseudonym 'The Brother of Low Degree' (James 1.9 A.V.). The first edition of the daily confessions appeared in 1957 and the second in 1998, and it bore the title *Cudd Fy Meiau*, quoting a well known Welsh hymn which echoed Psalm 18.12 (A.V.).

The central theme of the book is Pennar's spiritual journey which he reveals with astonishing candour. It is, however, important to recognize that he was writing fully aware of the realities of the world and Wales in the 1950s and there are references to some of these; he also writes lovingly and honestly about family matters. But his main purpose, and achievement, was his desire to bare his inner struggles – especially the struggles between flesh and spirit, between Nature and Grace – and reveal how a person could commune with God. I am not aware of such an honest and brave attempt in recent times – but I could be mistaken. Of course, there is inevitably an aura of self-regard about publishing such confessions and voices were raised at the time of their publication in *Y Tyst* doubting the wisdom of the venture. However, such protestations can be placed at the door of the prurience that affected sections of Nonconformity at the time. The integrity of Pennar cannot be doubted and the sheer honesty with which he reveals his inner thoughts and inclinations is striking. At a time when most Christians were still attached to a church life which owed so much to the nineteenth century, he is acutely aware of the crises facing them. And yet, he persevered as a principal, training theological students, until his retirement.

He rued the fact that he and his family were often impoverished and it is certain that he could have found satisfying academic roles at a number of universities or colleges. But he had a deep stubbornness of conviction which belied his genial and amiable nature. He declined to attend an interview, to which he had been invited, at Mansfield College, Oxford, for the chair of church history which had become vacant on Cadoux' death, 'on the grounds that he felt his vocation lay in Wales'. His commitment to Wales and the Welsh language was only second to his commitment to Christ – he himself would have seen it as one commitment. But there is equally no doubt about his internationalism. He married Rosemarie, who had been encouraged to flee Nazi Germany by her father because, although she was a Lutheran by faith, she had Jewish origins. He retained contact with a number of friends from various countries until the end of his life. His vast knowledge of literature and art made him receptive to many voices from many countries. His linguistic skills were extensive and his reading, together with his formidable memory, were astonishing.

He also had a surpassing knowledge of the Bible and of recent biblical scholarship. The direct references in *Diary of a Soul* total 98 – mostly from the four gospels but there are also wider biblical resonances. I have listed most of the former in the notes at the end of the book. One of the most striking features of the diary is the frequency of prayer and the manner in which God or Jesus is approached. These prayers constitute what is known in Welsh as *saeth weddïau*, that is unpremeditated, direct, immediate prayers (literal translation 'arrow prayers'). There are 76 in all and some of these – as in the entries for 13 and 20 September – provide us with some of the most moving passages of the book. While his prayers do not omit concern for others, in the nature of confession Pennar searches the hidden recesses of his soul and it is inevitable that he is poignantly personal. He addresses God in unusual ways in many of the prayers but, this does not detract from their value.

R Tudur Jones writes, 'On reading *Diary of a Soul* one can see what worries and temptations troubled Pennar. He yearned for clear signs of the presence of God and Christ. Another topic which arises often is the wholeness/oneness of everything that exists. The question is, how can "creation be made whole"... He opposes all dualism and that explains the strong desire to embrace everything and everybody within a comprehensive unity. This also explains his tolerant spirit towards a large number of individuals and opinions.'[3]

More – much, much more – could be said about Pennar Davies. For example, comment on his pacifist activities, his political involvements, his courageous support for the Welsh language, his brilliant short stories and his rich and exacting poetry, his novels, his historical writing, his translations, his preaching and lecturing, his literary criticisms and reviews, his articles and essays on a wide range of subjects. But these must await a comprehensive biography in English.

*

This translation has been undertaken as a sign of affection for one who was my tutor for three years in church history, and who always lectured in an even-handed but rigorous way about all the vagaries of that subject. He hid his light under a bushel and as students we were only dimly aware of his polymath qualities. His reserved, even shy, manner made him an enigmatic figure to many. (I can even claim that I was one of the first to discover the identity of the anonymous author when I had coffee with him and innocently inquired who he could possibly be, only to see consternation reflected on his face!) He officiated at my ordination and a month later at my wedding.

He, perhaps graciously, thought the best of everyone and gave the impression of a kindly disposition with his ever-ready smile; although, as the diary reveals, this could be a cover for a writhing anger which he had learned to control. There was an enigmatic aspect to his character, summed up by his minister, the Rev. F M Jones, during his funeral service in Swansea: '*Cudd Fy Meiau* is a cottage window in a mansion which is expansive in its architecture and its opulence, and perhaps it is there that we come closest to knowing Dr Pennar. But we shall continue to conjecture. And he will continue to smile on us.'

Professor Geoffrey Nuttall, a leading church historian and a friend of Pennar, wrote of him, 'His personality was like no one else's. I could call it enigmatic... but I prefer to say *complexio oppositorum*... Discussion left me sure there was a strong unity in him, embracing the puzzling opposites. If only I could find it; but I never did... Dear Pennar, keep us guessing... I hear him chuckle still.'[4]

*

I have endeavoured to be faithful to the original text in my translation rather than interpret it. Certain Welsh words and idioms are notoriously awkward to translate – for example, the most important distinction between *gwybod* i.e., to know, to understand, to appreciate; and *adnabod* i.e., to acknowledge, to recognize, to claim a relationship with someone. 'To know' is the usual translation of both words, whereas the distinction is important, especially in talking of the relationship between man and God and one's fellow man (which is *adnabod*), and occurs a number of times in *Diary of a Soul*: I have usually attempted a paraphrase. Translations of hymns are notoriously difficult but I have tried to retain their meanings without, alas, maintaining their poetry. At one point (2 November) I have taken the liberty of translating mediaeval Welsh words into English to ease comprehension.

Herbert Hughes
April 2011

Acknowledgements

My thanks are due to the following:

The United Reformed Church, The Union of Welsh Independents, The College of the Welsh Independents and a number of individuals for their generosity in helping to fund this venture.

To Pennar Davies's family for their support and encouragement.

To the Very Reverend Rowan Williams, Archbishop of Canterbury, for his perceptive introduction.

To the Rev. Dr D Densil Morgan for his reading of the initial manuscript.

To the Rev. Derwyn Morris Jones for his guidance and support.

To the Summer School of Welsh Independent Ministers for their encouragement.

To *Gwasg y Lolfa* for ensuring a publication worthy of Pennar.

Diolch i chi i gyd.

PREFACE

(To the first edition by Pennar Davies)

This diary was written during the year 1955 and published weekly in *Y Tyst** under the nom-de-plume 'The Brother of Low Degree'. I thank the editor for his support and patience and for the opportunity to publish the work as a volume and I would also like to thank the office of the Welsh Independents for a great deal of assistance. I am grateful to Mrs Curig Davies and to the Rev. Glyn Richards for their help in the task of correcting the proofs.

Important as are faith and prayer and worship in the lives of the Welsh, there has not been much enquiry into the secret places of 'the inner life'; at least if there have been enquirers, they have been reluctant to publish the fruits of their search. But the Diary is not an attempt to fill the gap; it is an attempt rather to dissect the disease of this poor man and to seek healing. The way of purification, the way of enlightenment, the way of unity – this is the pattern of experience of many of the brothers of the Anointed. It is only the way of purification that is described here. Confession has been painful for the diarist; any pain that he causes the reader must be forgiven him.

* This is the denominational paper of the Congregationalists/ Independents in Wales.

CHAPTER 1

THE BEGINNING OF THE YEAR

1 January (Saturday)

Some people think that it is foolhardy to keep a diary, and I believe there is a lot of truth in that supposition. But it is not true of all diaries. I attempted to keep diaries before, but the most successful one lasted no more than a few months. Observing the world was the purpose of that diary. Now I intend keeping another diary for a little while, and its purpose will be to study God, and to praise him, and to apply myself to his service: God in Christ and God embracing me through His Spirit.

Tonight, before retiring to bed, I led the family service at a home which had seen the internment of loved ones during the year, and as I led in prayer I heard the sighing of an elderly widow. Death: how can we explain it apart from God?

2 January (The Lord's Day)

It was fine this morning, although it was cold. When she heard the birds singing so serenely in the sunlight, the old widowed lady repeated a piece of ancient wisdom: 'If they sing before Candlemas they'll weep before Saint David's Day.' I showed an interest in the old saying – it is obviously older than denominationalism – and the dear lady added another saying, which was more encouraging: 'Candlemas will come, St David's Day will come, the holy God will come and every goodness.'

21

The holy God and every goodness! Here is true wisdom: seeing the variety and richness of the seasons, birds and fish and trees and flowers and the occasional cloud in a blue sky and a cloud of flies on the banks, and seeing every goodness and the holy God in everything. This is very near the heart of the wisdom of the ancient Welsh: seeing all of life as one and seeing in every form and colour and leap signs of the Presence.

I preached, somewhat nervously, to a small congregation in an exceedingly small meeting house in the morning and evening; and during the evening service I received a two-month-old child, under the sign of the water, to the privileges of the Church's fellowship. On the baby's face also I saw the holy God and every goodness. Without losing the consciousness of sin the principle of seeing God in the faces of His little ones must be nurtured. Our life on earth is defiled, but life in its essence is good.

3 January (Monday)

In the prayer meeting tonight one brother said that zealous Christians were too busy on Sundays to be with God. There is some truth in that. It is difficult *to pray* the Lord's Prayer when leading a congregation in the task of reciting it. The mechanics of worship, even in the simplest forms of ordinary worship, are often a hindrance to worship. I feel myself closer to God in the everyday tasks of life. And yet how often I have leapt from the plain to the mountain of his holiness under the influence of a sermon or during the intensity of the communion. How often in a quiet service Jesus has put his hand on mine.

4 January (Tuesday)

The new school term began today and the house was surprisingly quiet without the children. I had an opportunity during the morning to meditate without interruption for a little while, and the Comforter came close to me. This experience is difficult to describe: being aware of the presence of the Great Being not as a visitor from the Eternal Realm but as the Life of the World, and that Life – the Life of lives and the Spirit of spirits – striving against all evil, purifying, cleansing, burning and enlightening. How lovely is His nearness: the great Worker, and the remains of sweat and dirt and blood on his holy Hands.

5 January (Wednesday)

Every misfortune happened today: a day of accidents and misunderstanding and loss of temper and of losing one another. Living is difficult: living together is more difficult. One must learn to choose words more thoughtfully. None of us lives far from Bedlam; thank God that Bethlehem is near also. It is pleasant to think that I turned to God and leant on him when temptation came to strike and hurt.

> *Father of all comfort and the Lord of all mysteries, let us rest in you in all the struggles and afflictions of our little lives. Anoint our tongues and hands in Christ Jesus. Amen.*

6 January (Thursday)

One of the causes of our difficulties yesterday was our poverty. It still troubles us today. Following the happy expenditures of Christmas, the start of the new year is barren. This is a funny turn, but for the family of a poor minister it is serious. I know that many ministers are poorer than I am, and it is a mystery how they manage to keep body and soul together. Even if we manage to pay our way it can be certain that there is not a penny left over.

It is apparent that the call to the ministry today is a call to a degree of Holy Poverty. I have been reading 'The Little Flowers of Saint Francis' during the Christmas holidays, and the old emphasis on Holy Poverty as a divine calling is found there occasionally. Of course, Holy Poverty in the company of itinerant brothers is a great deal easier than Holy Poverty in the company of a wife and children. The poverty which ministers face in Wales today is holier poverty than anything which monks had to face. And it certainly has its glory. In the age of fat pay packets and the betrayal of convictions and ideals for the sake of profit and honours, the quiet courage of the minister and his wife raising a family with thrift and dignity on a pittance is not without its lustre. All praise, especially to the women, and my wife among their number, for the miracles which they perform. What a quiet joy in the heart to see the children growing and the home, despite every trouble and worry, being still a home.

But the whole, every hour, must be consecrated to God.

7 January (Friday)

There has been enough praying – of a kind – during the Week of Prayer. We are saying too much to God and not listening enough to him.

> *O Lord Saviour, open our hearts to receive your Christ. Prevent our hands from hurting him. Breathe your compassion on us. Amen.*

8 January (Saturday)

One thought has been pressing on my spirit today: thinking of God's need. He knows what poverty is. His glory is to share the need of One between the myriads. Is not that Creation? Is not that the Atonement? Is not that heaven?

9 January (The Lord's Day)

God the Almighty – and the All-impoverished. The gracious and comforting Father was close to me in the pulpit today. During recent years I have had many blessings from thinking that it is by living that we pray. Living for God, living with God – that is prayer, and it is only that way that one can pray without ceasing. The prayerful life in its quintessence does not consist of devotional exercises at particular times and following more or less formal patterns, but living for God and living with God. Thinking, working, playing, doing everything with a view to God's purpose and with an appetite for his austere love and his revolutionary presence – that is the essence of prayer. Eating, sleeping, dressing, tidying, washing, conversing, meeting one's fellow men, observing the events of the age, devoting oneself to good causes, doing the daily tasks and every other additional task, and in all of these to depend on God and give him glory and know that He is with you – that is prayer.

There is a blessing also in the ordinary devotional practices; there is a blessing in the act of summarising prayerful thoughts in the form of words and sentences. But these are poor things without *living* in the work and fellowship of the Lord. Brother Lawrence[1] is correct with his emphasis on the practice of the Presence of God at all times, in every task. Laying hold of the consciousness of the presence of God – that is delight, that is strength, that is wealth – and enjoying the experience consistently, perpetually, from morning to night, and sleeping, even, in the Eternal Arms – that is blessedness and glory. But the Christian must excel even over Brother Lawrence in one thing. For he states once that the troubles and unpleasant things of the world should be avoided, but the wayfarers of the Lord must face these things – face everything with Jesus, with God. To shut out the world to realize the presence of God is the tradition of the cloister; but the complete Christian life is to be with God in the world.

Thanks to Brother Lawrence, nevertheless, for confirming for me the practice of the Presence of God.

Strangely enough, I've had some difficulty in realizing the presence of God in the act of preaching. The preacher has to think of the details of the service and has to face a congregation and think of the message and the sections and words of the sermon; and although he knows that God is with him he is not always aware of His close touch and of the breath of his friendship. But today, the Father was very close, and the little pulpit was full of him. I was enabled to sit on the Throne of the Lamb today.

But I am not worthy. What shall I do?

10 January (Monday)

I have been thinking today about my unworthiness. The old self-accusation came to my heart: 'I am a man of unclean lips, and I dwell among people of unclean lips.'[2]

Sin lurks in my heart like dust in a house. The dust is difficult to bear, and to clean the house thoroughly is painful. The easy way of dealing with the dust is to tidy the occasional spot which shows up the dirt fairly clearly and to sweep a considerable amount of rubbish under the carpet.

There is no more unmistakeable sign of sin than the reluctance to acknowledge sin; and that reluctance impedes my fingers as I write these words.

One of the blessings of this diary may be that I will have to face my own sin.

11 January (Tuesday)

I had a busy day today. I became conscious of God's presence many times, but this awesome pleasure was sporadic rather than continuous. And shame was part of the experience also.

Once, I felt that the eye of God the Father was observing the postures of my soul, and that I was unclean in his sight. All the busyness could not cause me to throw aside this feeling of shame.

12 January (Wednesday)

Before retiring last night I tried to think of the forgiveness of God rather than my own faults. Into my imagination came a picture of Jesus upon the Cross. I heard in my heart his prayer of forgiveness for the murderers of Calvary. But in attempting to gaze at the divine tenderness of his eyes I saw the Consuming Fire.

For the unclean heart forgiveness is judgement.

13 January (Thursday)

I had an opportunity to play a little with the children this afternoon. Previously, many times, I felt a kind of pride on seeing the eldest son smiling at me with love and admiration (although he is full of mischief and fun and can say some things that are most irreverent). His father is a considerable hero for him at the moment. That is the way of things with children apparently. Perhaps another period will come before long, and his father will be least of all in his sight. But at the moment I am a hero to the boy, and usually this gives pleasure. But today I feel unworthy – unworthy of his admiration and unworthy of the honour of being a father.

I recall him saying about three years ago that his father was the best man in the world. And after considering for a while he added: 'I expect that God is better, but he ought to be: he is a lot older than Daddy.'

Oh Merciful God, Oh Sun which radiates goodness and purity, look on me with pity. Subdue every sin within me. Strengthen me to stride out against every evil which corrupts my soul. Draw my heart nearer to Your Heart, and let me come to you joyfully and willingly. Give your help in Christ the Lord. Amen.

14 January (Friday)

I was surprised today by the whiteness of the snow on the fields.

This is beauty; the white world is a surprise every time it comes. A big thank you is due to the snow for giving a new appearance to everything, and for causing us to reconsider field and mountain. But everything else that is white appears dirty and grey compared with the covering of snow. A little while back I was admiring the whiteness of the wool on the mountain sheep; now their whiteness appears shamefully imperfect.

I am ashamed when I compare my negligible goodness with the brilliant Goodness which is pure Light.

CHAPTER 2

THE ACCUSER

15 January (Saturday)

I spent a day today with the Accuser, and I tried to defend myself. It is difficult for me now to put into words many of the thoughts that I had. I know that I told my Accuser that I was a better man than many of my contemporaries. God forgive me.

The Accuser spoke not a word, but his silence was deafening.

I tried to prove that I was fairly good, and that I could be better except for my circumstances. I am more generous than so-and-so, for example; and I could be even more generous if I had this world's riches. I am more industrious than some: that is what I have been told more than once. And although so many things have been neglected by me, is that my fault? After all, I am only a creature of flesh and blood. It is the flesh that is weak. The spirit is more than willing. I am clean-living according to the standards of the world. At least my name looks respectable on a letter of commendation. And if my self-discipline is not perfect, am I to blame? Have I not inherited a wild nature? Were not the circumstances of my upbringing unfortunate with a view to the need for taming it? I was given an unmanageable nature and I was not given every opportunity to cultivate it. Considering everything, it is a miracle that I am as good as I am.

The Accuser did not say anything, but looked at me until I hid my eyes with my hands.

After I have written as much as this in my diary it is easy to see the rot which is as close as ever to my soul.

And yet it is in the Faith that I live, and I know that I have had the fellowship of God and his Christ and his Spirit many times. I dare not deny that. But there are ravines and the occasional plain in my personality that have not been completely possessed by the Saving Grace.

16 January (The Lord's Day)

The Accuser was at my elbow during the morning service, but I have no doubt about his presence during the evening service.

Who is the Accuser?

17 January (Monday)

Sometimes I think that the Accuser is Jesus – Jesus and all who belong to him throughout the ages. Every courage, every purity, every mercy – all of these have allied with the Accuser against me.

At other times I feel that the Accuser is the Great Enemy, belittling and exposing me, and his derisory laughter distressing my heart.

Who are you, the strong Accuser? Come to me, for me to wrestle with you. Will I receive a blessing from you? Can I struggle with you, until I hear your voice saying, 'Let me go; daylight is coming?'[1] *Accuser, come to me. I will not let you go, unless you bless me.*

18 January (Tuesday)

I was deeply troubled by a nasty dream last night, and the nightmare remained with me throughout the day.

I dreamt that I and others lived in a large lonely house. Refugees came to me, and received refuge from me in my house, people who had fled from some great Hitlerian persecution. One of the women in this company had a pistol. Someone – I do not recall who – gave me a pistol also. I looked upon the devilish weapon in terror; it was completely impossible for me to use it. I felt a desire to be rid of it. Instead, I put it in a drawer. We were all afraid that the servants of the cruel persecution would fall upon us to incarcerate or kill us. But happy news came to us: the tyranny had been overcome. A feast was arranged to celebrate the liberation. But in the middle of the feast the door opened and two cruel, vengeful, merciless villains came in – representatives of the persecution, and their aim was to torture and kill us. The woman raised her pistol, but the two wretches had murderous weapons. I ran through another door to the drawer in the next room. One of the two followed me. Trembling, I got hold of my pistol. We both fired at the same time.

I woke up frightened. I do not know what a psychiatrist would say about this dream but I am convinced of one thing. It was not fear of being killed that frightened me but disgust and dread of the act of attempting to kill another.

There is in me some self-hatred. 'I am a man of unclean lips'. And although I hate war and reject everything that is associated with it, I feel today that my hands are red with blood.

It is not often that I have as memorable a dream as this.

19 January (Wednesday)

This is a busy week and I have to spend much of my time away from home. 'Activity', some say. 'Too many irons in the fire', others say. The accusing thought comes to me that all this busyness can be an excuse for being spiritually lazy.

'Every man should examine himself'.[2] Attending committees and conferences could be easier than this. It is possible to expend time and energy endlessly without serving God.

Being active is not an absolute virtue. There are some people who work from morning to night to make money.

Serving Mammon can take as much time as serving God.

How much work do I accomplish for God?

20 January (Thursday)

The monks previously were very conscious of the sin called 'accidia': a lack of zeal and a lack of perseverance in God's service. For many it was spiritual aridity in devotion: the mind wandering in prayer and a certain emptiness perpetually troubling the soul, and disgust at the limitations of the 'religious' life unsettling the spirit.

I do not think of devotion and prayer and 'religion' in that way. The road I try to tread is to be with God by living and working and playing among men. But this means doing everything to His glory – 'seek firstly the kingdom of God'.[3] That is the aim. The meaning of spiritual laziness is forgetting or avoiding the aim.

I am beginning to tire of the presence of the Accuser.

'Seek firstly'. Do I seek God's Kingdom first?

Is it God or myself that I wish to glorify?

21 January (Friday)

Oh Lord of all work, grant me zeal in the work you have given me. Give me a willing heart. I only exist to glorify you. Make me a servant, for you too are a servant. You clothe the lily and give sustenance to the crow. You are a servant to the fine sand and the stars. You rule through Your service. Rule, oh Lord, in me. Amen.

22 January (Saturday)

I sometimes feel that I am a small part of a great machine which is always working, and every wheel and piston and pin are in motion. In that sense, I am extremely industrious. But this world is the machine, and in the eyes of the world the highest virtue of every part is to conform with the machine.

To what degree is our 'religious' life a component of the machine of the world?

Conferences, committees, societies for promoting every kind of good cause: these things are necessary. We are thankful for them. God help me to serve better on them. But may God save me also from involvement so completely in them that I fail to see the Lord sitting on a high and exalted throne, and fail to see His purpose for me in the crisis of the age, and fail to utter the words: 'Here I am. Send me'.[4]

23 January (The Lord's Day)

I felt today that the glory of the Gospel is too much for me.

On reading the words I wrote in my diary yesterday I see that I am in danger of putting the health of my own soul above those activities which help me and others in ushering Christ's salvation into the realm of the world.

God save me from the 'pious' forms of self-seeking.

It is my conviction that no one will be saved except that all will be saved.

Thank God also for the 'All in all' which is promised to us.

How can anyone be completely saved while those he loves are lost in the world?

God is indeed 'satisfied', satisfied with the work of His Christ on the Cross. But in another sense, he is 'dissatisfied' until he can gather all His people back to his breast.

An all embracing salvation is offered to us in Christ. 'And when I am lifted up from the earth, I will draw everyone to myself.'[5] He is still there, and will remain there until the last wretch has come to him: 'Until the full complement of the nations comes. And then all of Israel shall be saved.'[6]

The joy of Heaven is not complete while one sinner is unrepentant. Salvation is never perfected for anyone as long as the most insignificant brother remains in the darkness and cold.

It is not by himself that a man is saved.

24 January (Monday)

Oh Father God, let me serve You more completely. Without You I am nothing. Fill the emptiness within me. Teach me, for the sake of the

Crucified, to give you my all. Do not allow me to keep anything back.
Save me to save more to the glory of the Name which is above every
name.

25 January (Tuesday)

I am not adequate.
I am not sufficient.

26 January (Wednesday)

'Who is sufficient?'[7] is one of the great questions of scripture.
There is comfort in it. But by itself it does not remove my
responsibility for my own failings. I would rather forget them
for a little while but that is not the way to conquer them.

I tried to pray more earnestly today and to read portions
of scripture relevant to my condition. The Gospel is full of
comfort to the person who repents. But I feel that there are
depths of failure in me of which I have not yet fully repented.

For me, today, the Bible is full of accusations.

27 January (Thursday)

It was a relief for me to have to leave home this afternoon.
In chatting with my friend on the road and discussing the
future of the Christian ministry in Wales, I felt (despite the
bitterness of the complicated issues) that I was escaping from
myself.

This has been a busy and distressful day, but the Accuser
– and the Saviour also – have withdrawn somehow.

28 January (Friday)

Last night in bed, away from home, I failed to sleep for a few
hours.

But by some unexpected grace, my discomfort was
overpowered by a great comfort. I do not know yet whether I
have fully repented, but repentance of some kind was certainly
part of the experience.

It came to my mind, as I tried to sleep, those great words

in John's Gospel: 'My Father is always working, and I too must work.'[8]

I felt like a man in a boat who failed to row against the wind but was propelled by a benign current; and I became conscious, as I had previously, of the presence of the Great Worker. I saw my insignificant work as part of the immense Work of the whole universe – and my failures as trivial, temporary hindrances which will be the object of laughter to the Workers when the Work is finished.

In the darkness and silence I was conscious of a certain rhythm – the rhythm of creation, the heart of God beating. I knew that the Breath of God was in the room. I was enabled to rest in the infinite Energy, the invincible Strength, the gracious Power which is from eternity to eternity, annihilating annihilation, creating and guiding and preserving.

I prayed, without words. If I were to put the prayer into words it would be something like this:

My Father, my Brother, my Heart! Forgive every weakness and every profligacy which is in me. You are the strong, unprofligate Worker. Possess your servant. Fill my life with your hope; guide my life with your wisdom. Give me work, and work in me. For your name's sake. Amen.

And in the noise of the Heartbeat of every heart I went to sleep.

How pleasing it was to arrive home tonight and receive the welcome of my dearest.

Demiurge is a strange name for the Creator, and the original meaning of that word was 'worker for the people'. There has been a great deal of fanciful theologizing amongst the cognoscenti of the early Christian centuries concerning this demiurge. A worker for the people: God never fails to provide a good example for his saints.

It is a joy to have fellowship with the Worker and the Exalted Peasant.

CHAPTER 3

THE WORKER AND PATERFAMILIAS

29 January (Saturday)

This has been a day of joy. I am so grateful that I have had the grace to think about the Greatest Worker in the midst of my dissatisfaction with myself and my piffling work.

When I was reading and praying and preparing today I tried to think of the wonderful work which goes on around us. What riches there are in the Psalms about Nature and her wonders. 'The heavens', 'the moon and stars', 'sheep and cattle and wild animals too', 'the birds and the fish and the creatures in the seas'.[1] That is work – the suns sailing through the void; the worlds turning; the creatures flying, walking, swimming; the species striving and changing; the plants growing and flowering and bearing fruit; and every blade of grass and every insect and every unit of life overflowing with secret energy. Work! An ant heap is something of a mystery; those things that occur in the human body are even more mysterious. And the deeper we probe into the secrets of the universe, the greater the mystery and the terror.

Movements, shapes, innumerable activities – and all is work. The meaning of the universe is work, and God is active in everything.

What is work but movements and efforts with a purpose to them?

30 January (The Lord's Day)

I suppose that every preacher sometimes feels that he is crying in the wilderness, with only stones to listen to him. I felt differently today. I felt that the whole strength of creation was behind the Gospel – and more than that, much more: all the strength of the Creator. After all, the New Testament takes a fairly optimistic view of man despite his failure and corruption. It takes quite an optimistic view even of stones. When he condemns man's sin, Jesus says: 'God can take these stones and make descendants for Abraham'.[2]

31 January (Monday)

I don't believe that I have ever had the experience of being lost in God. Some of the mystics have had the experience – being lost in God like a drop of water being lost in the sea. Sometimes I use the words 'being lost' – in my public prayers for instance – but it is obvious that I do not mean anything like that experience, the experience of a drop in the sea.

Nevertheless, I have had the experience more than once that I was part of the Godhead; not lost like a drop in the sea, but part of him like a theme or one little note can be part of a great symphony. The note is not lost in the symphony; on the contrary it is its rightful place. And yet it is part of the whole composition, and without the whole it would be meaningless.

This feeling of being part of the Godhead remained with me today. I thought of the great work of creation and all the creatures, and as myself as part of the whole.

Oh God, oh Infinity, oh Father, oh Benefactor, oh Almighty Energy, oh Invincible Love, I cannot ask for a greater blessing than that my life be part of Your Life. Give me Your Spirit in Christ Jesus. Amen.

1 February (Tuesday)

In one sense, and in a profoundly evangelical sense, no one can be lost in the Godhead. We are lost without him.

It is in Him we are at Home.

2 February (Wednesday)

This afternoon it was enjoyable to watch my two sons playing. They do not often play together, since the elder one plays horsemen and cowboys and the younger one enjoys pulling a wooden train across the floor.

We, their father and mother, have given the children pet names. This is a kind of family joke. And occasionally, these names have proved very useful when the children's affairs were being discussed in their presence without them knowing. This is an old custom among parents. I shall use the comic names in this diary.

'McTavish' has always been an eager, mischievous boy, moving swiftly from enthusiasm to enthusiasm. During the weeks before Christmas he will change his mind every day about the presents he would like to have. I never saw anyone who gleans so much fun from playing with his friends.

He shows his affection in play rather than in kissing and embracing. It is a pleasure to tell him a story and to try and tell it in a dramatic manner. He will listen avidly and respond with feeling and animation to every exciting happening in it. He has also the flaws that come from having excitable emotions.

His little brother, 'Ap Siencyn', is totally different. It is too early yet to say what he will be like in years to come. To strangers he gives the impression of being more loveable than McTavish. He likes climbing on to people's laps and embracing them gently. And to be fair, I believe his amiability is wholly sincere. But I have never seen such bottomless stubbornness in a child. Correction has a great effect on McTavish: he will either lose his temper or break his heart, one or the other. But Ap Siencyn's response to correction is the most uncooperative stubbornness imaginable. When he was younger, he would commit all kinds of rash misdeeds, like wandering from home, running on to a busy street, locking doors and hiding the keys, and it was impossible to discipline him. Mercifully time has tamed his indomitable spirit.

It is funny to see them playing together – like a quick squirrel and a suspicious hedgehog. They will quarrel by the end.

They will have to mature before learning to play together. They cannot be compelled to play together, although they can be reconciled and led.

Goodness cannot be forced.

Before I was married and had children I imagined that children could be easily nurtured by making rules and forcing the children to keep them. By now, as far as this goes, I am a wiser man. Every rule and command is in vain without a healthy relationship between parents and their children. Without this relationship the home ceases to be a home and becomes a prison or a desert.

All of us have our Home in God. In His Providence the Eternal Paterfamilias nurtures His children, teaching us to play together and work together and live together, creating the beneficent relationship between Him and us and between one another.

3 February (Thursday)

Rumour of war comes from the Far East. Every bully shouts so loudly that it becomes difficult for many to hear the cry of the Eternal Peacemaker.

To you, the Peacemaker who is from eternity, I wish to turn to, now and in every crisis. Save us from fear, from self-righteousness, from falsehood, from destruction. Through the Crucified. Amen.

4 February (Friday)

My wife enjoys chatting about the children while she is ironing their clothes.

There is Motherhood in the Godhead also. Who is it that irons the White Raiments of Heaven?

5 February (Saturday)

I fear that I am neglecting the task of searching the recesses of my heart and conscience. The Accuser came to confuse my prayers this morning.

Grace, Mercy, Forgiveness – I know that there is more than enough available. But I also know that I have not tasted all which has been allotted to me.

6 February (The Lord's Day)

There was a lovely promise of spring in the air this morning.

Grace, Mercy, Forgiveness – those were the themes of my sermons morning and evening. I believe passionately in the Divine Love. A powerful wave of the Great Love came over my soul before I finished the sermon in the evening. It was difficult to continue speaking.

The greatest privilege given to man is to live in the Divine Love. The second privilege is to preach it.

Woe to the man who preaches the Gospel without living it.

Oh Paradigm of every goodness, my Father, my Mother, my Brother, my Friend and the Blood of my heart, make me like Yourself in Christ Jesus. Amen.

It is one thing to believe in the Divine Love. It is another to perfect oneself in it.

7 February (Monday)

How many Christians in Wales use their hymn book as an assistance to personal devotion? Most of the time I receive more of a blessing from the hymn book than from any 'prayer book'. It is possible that this betrays a lack of discipline in my devotional life, but that's how it is.

I sometimes feel that the greatest hymn of all in Welsh is 'Here is love like all the oceans' by Gwilym Hiraethog.[3] I have heard many claim that Isaac Watts' hymn 'When I survey the wondrous Cross' is the greatest, and that is probably true as far as English hymnody is concerned. But of the two hymns, 'Here is love' and 'When I survey', it is impossible to say that one is superior to the other. Watts' hymn has the cry of the individual's soul before the Cross, seeing in the Cross the wondrous Love which demands 'my soul, my life, my all'. Hiraethog's hymn portrays the highest miracle of the universe: the whole meaning of the Providence of the Most High becomes evident on Calvary, and salvation pours over the world.

On Calvary all the fountains of the deep are rent; all the dams of heaven which were whole until now have broken. Grace and love poured down here like a flood, and pure righteousness and peace will kiss a guilty world.

Here is glory. The salvation occurs in the individual soul in Watts' hymn; it is in the universe and in society that we see the miracle according to Hiraethog's great vision. Both truths are essential, and, indeed, they are one.

The emphasis of 'When I survey' has been more acceptable than the other one to many Christians during recent centuries. The emphasis of 'Here is love' is needed if the human race is to survive the atomic age.

8 February (Tuesday)

I gave a few hours yesterday afternoon and today to a campaign which involves visiting the homes of strangers. There is comfort in having good company for work such as this, as in open air work. I was surprised to see so much goodwill among the people, especially among those who are not very wealthy. It is obvious that we must bring the Gospel directly to individuals and speak with them at their homes.

9 February (Wednesday)

I have been thinking of Jesus' pure and dedicated conduct:

> Oh great and exalted Jesus, give of Your pure nature
> To a feeble and weak person in a barren land.[4]

There has been more than one attempt to draw some 'rule and exercise for holy living' from what is known of his life and behaviour. This is a rather dangerous endeavour.

Some have emphasized fasting and prayer practices and the unmarried state and the poverty and the spiritual communion in the isolation of Nature –

> The Man who loved the mountain
> And the solitude of fields at night.[5]

– and it was from this emphasis that monasticism and ascetic living grew. This is an over-emphasis of some of the outward aspects of Jesus' life. Those who pursued these aspects forgot that the Gospels present the life of Jesus as something which is totally different to the ascetic life of John the Baptist. The Good News is something to be enjoyed to the full – that was life for Jesus, and he did not expect his disciples to follow the severe practices of John. He offended many of his religious contemporaries by eating and drinking, and eating and drinking often in the company of the disreputable. There is nothing 'ascetic' in his poverty and work. These originated in his being the Son of God and his saving mission and his evangelical values.

On the other hand, the life of Jesus is very different from the picture of him that was formed in the imagination of the romantic poets and the liberal theologians. For these he was the apostle of the natural life and of the open air, a man who challenged the narrow standards of his age, a man who broke the rules by cherishing the glory of man and earth, a man who desired freedom for the inherent goodness of human nature.

The truth is that the Lord Jesus Christ was, and is, a saviour. He could see the true glory of man and earth – he could also see their need, he could see their corrupt condition, he could see that they were without hope apart from the Great Sacrifice.

His personal life is, therefore, a pattern of freedom and

dedication – freedom from the shackles of imperfect, corrupt, enslaving standards, and of commitment to his saving work.

Freedom and dedication. To what degree does my personal life show that I belong to the Lord Jesus?

10 February (Thursday)

It is pleasant to meditate on Jesus in the days of his flesh: what he wrote on the earth, the hands that blessed the children, the feet which walked towards Jerusalem, the back that sank under the cross, the eyes which looked at the penitent thief, the head which bowed in death. I shall endeavour in meditation to draw near to him and look at the weals and scars on his skin and hear his breathing and his laughter and touch his hand.

He was a man of flesh and blood, and the Divine Love shining on every gesture and word, on every scowl and smile.

11 February (Friday)

Oh Lord Jesus, oh Splendour of the Eternal, oh Fellow Man, draw me close to Yourself. You are the Way, and the Truth, and the Life. Oh Wonder of the Ages, you desire to be our friend. Accept my hand into Your hand. I will go with You every step of the way. Amen.

CHAPTER 4

FREEDOM AND DEDICATION

12 February (Saturday)

The winter is not about to loosen its hold on us yet. I had to travel through the cold to keep an engagement on Sunday in a beloved and quite famous church; and on the way, as I was looking yet again in wonder at the whiteness of the snow, I meditated on the pure life of Jesus. Suddenly I became aware of the disturbing nearness of the Accuser.

To what degree is my personal life a reflection of the freedom and dedication portrayed in the Gospels?

13 February (The Lord's Day)

I preached this evening on the Incarnation, and the fruitful idea which is found in the New Testament that the powers of the Incarnation prevail in those whom the love of God in Christ unites in a holy family. The idea is too daring for many of the theologians: the Incarnation as a present fact. The Bible is much more daring than most of its commentators.

For some the whole idea of 'Imitatio Christi'[1] is too daring. But it is in the Gospel. We are called to follow Christ and to be perfect in his love. Of course, the guilty soul is horrified by the challenge, but we must face it. Being like Christ, being like God – that is the test.

I also fear the challenge. The freedom of Christ, freedom from everything which restricts our service and distorts our religion and life; the dedication of Christ, the commitment and self-discipline which are the conditions of God's saving work in our lives – to what extent can the freedom and commitment be seen in my life? Where do I fail?

14 February (Monday)

Christ is the Free Man. My soul, look at him, his nakedness, his blood, his sweat. The Eternal Prisoner! The soldiers beat him, swearing and laughing drunkenly. They feel that they represent a superior civilization to his and a richer culture and a far superior race. In every blow there is contempt and lust. Are not the soldiers of Rome the masters of the world?

Even in his agony and shame the Christ pities the soldiers in their captivity.

He is the Free Man. Look upon him, my soul. Does he have wealth, worldly power, an influential position in the organization of his country? No. He has nothing now but his body, and the soldiers treat the body as they wish. Flesh, blood, skin, bones, hair – these are the only things he now has, and the Kingdom of Darkness wants to take these things away from him.

Look upon him, my soul. He is a Free Man: the only free man in Jerusalem.

Pilate's empire is a prison; Caiaphas' religion is a prison; Judas' dream is a prison; Peter's confusion is a prison; Herod's ambition is a prison: Barabbas' revolutionary movement is a prison, although Barabbas has been released from his cell. Christ alone is free.

My soul, stand with him. There, at his side, under the soldiers' lash, freedom is to be found.

15 February (Tuesday)

I have been reading 'Jesus of Nazareth' by the poet Dyfed[2] and was blessed. I tried to meditate with him above the mystery of the Incarnation: The essence of heaven was lowered – the King was emptied of all value; over the cold ground of the grey earth the creator of the suns as a creature was seen. I noticed that his words about the Mother of Jesus – 'Behold a mother for a

Divine Being' – would be acceptable today to many along with the Pope. But there is something inevitable in the description of Mary 'with the King at her breasts', the description of the joy of the young Jesus among the beauties of nature – and the powers of Evil working at the same time even in the natural world preparing for the crucifixion:

> Nature so harmless,
> Invigorating the summer flowers;
> Clothing them with crowns
> Of heavenly colours to give him joy;
> But not knowing that the Evil One
> Was creating another crown,
> To be placed by a poor wretch
> As a painful mockery on his holy head.

Dyfed usually follows the traditional theology, with its emphasis on the Divinity of Christ rather than on his humanity, and that in the rhetorical manner which has given more than one striking piece of poetry in Welsh: 'Placing the thorns of judgement on the Crowned Head of the world'. But sometimes he strikes a different note:

> Needy in my distress – despite the anguish,
> I need not fear today;
> This mocked companion of mine
> I see as a Brother on Calvary.

The Crowned Head of the World as a brother; the King on the breasts. One must meditate a lot on this mystery, the mystery of the Incarnation. It is not by analysing that we gain understanding. That is the mistake of many theologians: analysing – forgetting the difference between mystery and puzzle. One must be in Christ to understand Christ; one has to be in the Incarnation to comprehend the Incarnation.

16 February (Wednesday)

Oh Lord Jesus Christ, I want to be with you.
   *I am trying to follow you. But I know that I cannot follow you
without complete dedication to your glorious cause. I feel that there
are many constraints holding me back, and I dread looking at them.
But I know that you, by stepping forward, expect me to follow you.*
   *Oh Lord Jesus, come back to smile on me, to tell me to be brave
and to follow you. Have mercy on me. You know me better than I
know myself. Give me your hand. Give me your hand.*

I saw, in my imagination, Jesus walking ahead of me to
Jerusalem. I was one of the disciples. I noticed that Peter was
walking silently by himself. Some of the disciples were talking
together quietly as they followed the Lord. James and John,
the sons of Zebedee, were sometimes telling them to quicken
their pace.

I tried in my imagination to see only Jesus. Indeed, I
attempted to hurry forward to be with him; but I was ever
conscious of the fears and doubts of the disciples.

By trying to pray in my heart I felt that I was failing on the
road. I lost sight of Jesus. The prayer died in my heart.

I failed to grasp again the picture which had excited my
imagination and had disappeared. I believe that I know to
some extent what is the meaning of being lost.

I am so impotent today.

17 February (Thursday)

is missing from the original edition

18 February (Friday)

'Can you drink the cup that I must drink? Can you be baptised
in the way I must be baptised?'[3]

19 February (Saturday)

Many Christians are in favour of outward aids to lead them into a closer and richer fellowship with the Lord Jesus. They pray before a crucifix, perhaps, and that bearing an image of the crucified Jesus. One of the dangers of this kind of worship is to think of the sufferings of the Cross and forget the Love which brought them and the Purpose which was fulfilled in them. This danger is also evident when looking on many of the renderings of the Crucifixion painted by artists. In the famous paintings by Grunewald, where there is plenty of spiritual passion and strength, there is a danger that we could see the bloody wounds of Jesus before we see the Love and Sacrifice. I believe that I have had a greater blessing by meditating on pictures which show Jesus doing his work among men, healing, blessing, calling. I know that it is all in the Cross, but the essence of the work of Jesus is Life and Joy, and in one sense, the portrayal of the Crucifixion is a failure unless it conveys first of all the Life and Joy.

One glorious painting of Jesus by Rembrandt comes often to my mind. I am amazed by the strength and gentleness. There is not one of the ritual images of the Godhead in the picture: only the splendour of the Adorable One himself.

But it is through my own imagination that the Spirit can best work. I try to imagine the face and body and hands. I try and look in the quick of Jesus' eye and see the beauty of his smile and gently hold his arms. And by doing this often I became acquainted with his appearance.

By now I recognize his cough, and I always see a small scar beneath his left eye.

And how lovely the face and voice. 'Oh speak, gentle Jesus.'[4]

20 February (The Lord's Day)

As I was leading the worship and preaching the Word, I became definitely conscious of the Presence in the evening service. The certainty came suddenly in the middle of the sermon: Jesus and his love. But as I prayed silently after the service I became aware of the Accuser.

I do not preach as freely and as courageously as I should. I do not preach without fear or favour. I sometimes soften my message to avoid offending someone.

One must be reasonable, one must be wise, they say. And I suppose they are right. But the truth will stand. And the preacher who tempers his message a little is in danger of distorting the truth to please his audience.

God save us from this.

It is true that many people know where I stand on many topics; and so they know that I, when talking of the love of Christ, mean something more than a soft feeling within me. And this is more effectual than endless repetition. (Am I excusing myself?) But plain speaking is sometimes necessary.

The voice of Jesus comes clearly and strongly over the centuries. 'Oh you unfaithful people! How long must I stay with you? How long do I have to put up with you?'[5]

21 February (Monday)

Oh Glorious Greatness, who exists before memory and before time, give us the Freedom of the Christ, the Freedom of the Holy Spirit, Your own Sovereign Freedom. I have no freedom except in Your service. You have freed me from the clay and dust, from the darkness of my mother's womb, and my foolish self-seeking. Free me now from every fear and every lovelessness. For Your name's sake. Amen.

22 February (Shrove Tuesday)

The season of Lent is about to begin. I am not attracted to the manner in which some observe the season. But it is not inappropriate for me to continue questioning myself.

And today the question is: Am I free?

'But the Lord is Spirit, and where the Lord's Spirit is present, there is freedom.'[6]

'Stand then in the freedom into which Christ freed us.'[7]

'He who looks on the perfect law of freedom and remains in it.'[8]

'In the hope that creation one day would be set free from its slavery to decay to share in the glorious freedom of the children of God.'[9]

23 February (Ash Wednesday)

I read in a prayer somewhere recently – in Ellis Wynne's translation of *The Rule and Exercises of Holy Living*,[10] I think – that God is free and that he is not bound except by the bonds of His own love.

I attempted to think of the temptation of Jesus in the desert. I tried to stand with him amidst the stones and on the top of the high mountain and on the pinnacle of the temple. I fear that I failed to stand with him. I must try again. And yet despite the barrenness of my meditation in one sense, I had a deeper impression than ever of the complete freedom of Jesus. He was the Lord – the Lord of the natural world, as he stood amidst the stones in the desert; the Lord of man's civilization, while he stood on the top of the high mountain looking at the kingdoms of the earth; the Lord of the spiritual world as he looked down from the pinnacle of the temple. He was free. He had the Freedom which creates, which saves and which rules.

24 February (Thursday)

To what degree are the lives of Christians enslaved like the lives of hypocrites such as the Pharisees in the past? For that is one of the differences between the morality of the Pharisees and the morality of Jesus, the difference between enslavement and freedom.

I recalled the last verse of a poem by W J Gruffydd, 'The Pharisee':[11]

All the pious Rabbis, when they talk to the children,
Raise him as a pattern of what is a Jew and a saint;
Temperance and living a life of thrift made him great,
But it was he who sent my Lord to Calvary.

To what extent are the virtues of the most respectable people in our churches like the virtues of the Pharisee – being negative, different, worldly, enslaved? And I (who once insisted that I was a free man in the moral world), to what degree am I a participant in this enslavement?

25 February (Friday)

We enjoyed our family life immensely this week. Anna, as dear as ever, came here, and the children welcomed her warmly: and she has come to stay. And we had the company of Branwen also, and 'Flanagan' – that is our jocular name for our little daughter – who commandeered her completely. The children were unusually gentle and happy.

But as I enjoyed the family happiness I could not but remember that the bonds of home life could also be restrictive. 'For whoever does the will of God, he is my brother, and sister, and mother.'[12] So said the Free Man.

26 February (Saturday)

I have been with Christ in the wilderness in my meditation, and I have tried to face the first temptation with him.

I tried to meditate with Jesus. 'The attitude you should have is the one that Christ Jesus had.'[13] Is not this close to the heart of Christian prayer? And are we not inclined to neglect this way of praying?

I watched him. He was sitting on a big stone, meditating intensely and making lines on the soil with a stick. He raised his head and gazed pensively on the desolate land.

I struggled to think with him: to think of food – in Palestine in the past, in Wales today; amongst the peoples of Arabia and Palestine and the ancient Roman world; in the countries of the

East and West in our troubled age. The need of man; the effort to subsist; famine and nakedness; greed and jealousy; children dying; crowds screaming; rulers conspiring – it all came to my mind, and something like pity entered my heart.

I looked in the eyes of my Fellow man. True pity was in them.

The strange words came to my lips: 'If you are the son of God, command these stones to turn into bread.'[14]

Jesus turned his head towards me and smiled.

I lost the thread of my meditation. I read again the blessed words from Mathew's Gospel: 'Human beings cannot live by bread alone, but need every word that God speaks.'[15]

27 February (The Lord's Day)

I preached tonight about prayer as a means not only of receiving spiritual strength but of pouring spiritual strength on other lives.

Pray until the perspiration flows: that is the only way to save a soul and a nation and a world. Every sermon that does not derive from prayer and immerses itself in prayer will fail. There was no Pentecost without an upper room.

Oh Holy Spirit, pray within me. Speak in me, Oh Christ. My Father, elevate my heart.

'In the same way the Spirit also comes to help us, weak as we are. For we do not know how we ought to pray; the Spirit himself pleads with God for us in groans that words cannot express.'[16]

28 February (Monday)

I have been thinking all day of the Temptation of Jesus. He has a wonderful freedom about him even in the crisis of the Temptation. In the desert, in the very high mountain, on the pinnacle of the temple – everywhere He is the Free Man, free to choose and free to choose the truth.

1 March (Tuesday, Saint David's Day)

I have been celebrating the day in the company of 'Welsh exiles' in England. There were bucketsful of nostalgia in the speeches, mixed with a plenitude of flattery to the local mayor. It was painful for all the guests to hear me say something about the condition of Wales today and the need to move politically to save our heritage. They looked appalled when I mentioned S O Davies's[17] bill to get a provincial parliament for Wales. Apart from one Nonconformist minister and one young man, there was not an atom of true love towards our Wales of today in her danger and opportunity. It is so easy to speak tearfully about the dear old village and the half-forgotten language, without being in the least aware of any sense of responsibility.

Neither was there much interest in the work of St David. I spoke of his aims and methods and tried to apply them to our situation today. I was thanked by someone for my sermon and my remarks were followed by selections of 'Desert Song'[18] being sung with passion by two members of the local opera company (one of them had some connection with Wales).

One of the members complained to me (a mother of a child who will this year be sitting the examination for entry to the grammar school) that the children of Wales would have an unfair advantage since a higher percentage of them would be allowed to go the grammar school, many more than in England. She said that she knew of 'exiled' Welsh families in England who send their children to live with grandmother or some aunt in Wales until they manage to enter the grammar school, and then, of course, transfer to the corresponding school in the locality in England where the parents live. 'The injustice must be removed,' she said, with righteous indignation and in strident English. 'Our children should have the same chance as the children of Wales.'

I don't know why I record such things as these in this diary. I only know that this 'celebration' made me profoundly glum.

2 March (Wednesday)

I had a restless night last night. I turned to pray and meditate. St David's picture rose in my mind – the holy life, the hill of the Gospel rising under his feet, patience and perseverance and gentleness overpowering enmity, and the joy of the awakening leaping from place to place in my beloved Wales. When I tried to pray with David I felt once more that I was breathing the air of the desert and Jesus himself was present.

Jesus was there, and the Great Enemy trying to deceive him by tempting him.

'Remember the needs of the body,' said the Tempter. 'Forget the needs of the soul. Food, clothes, education for the children, respectability, employment, wages, honours. Not for you alone, of course, but do not forget that you have as much right as everyone else. Indeed, you have more of a right. Are you not God's son?'

'Human beings cannot live on bread alone, but need every word that God speaks.'[19]

Suddenly Jesus withdrew from me, leaving the Enemy with me – and in me.

This evening I heard a sermon about the love of God and Christ. That is the purpose of life, and nothing else. But the Enemy is within me, gnawing and poisoning me.

3 March (Thursday)

The Enemy is within me. The Tempter is within me. The Accuser is within me.

4 March (Friday)

Oh Great Jesus, speak within me. Declare within me every word which comes from God's mouth. Wrestle with the Enemy within me. May his power and passion turn into glory to the Highest, now and evermore. Amen.

5 March (Saturday)

To what degree is the Christianity of the age partaking of the freedom of Jesus?

For Jesus the Pharisees were enslaved by the outer tyranny of the Law – the ceremonial laws and the moral laws of an extremely formal nature, and all far removed from God's righteousness. 'How terrible for you Pharisees. You give God a tenth of the seasoning herbs, such as mint and rue and all the other herbs, but you neglect justice and love for God.'[20] So according to Luke. And again in Mathew: 'How terrible for you, teachers of the Law and Pharisees! You hypocrites! You give to God a tenth even of the seasoning herbs, such as mint, dill and cumin, but you neglect to obey the really important teachings of the law, such as justice and mercy and honesty.'[21] That is an accusation that could be brought against much of our Christianity today.

There are Christian communities which expect their members to obey rules on fasting but feed their lust for making money through gambling; there are other communities who thunder against gambling but are silent or who vacillate when faced by the evil of war.

Our harmony of values is so imperfect and every system of values is so enslaving without the Spirit. That is the secret of the Lord's Freedom: it is the Freedom of the Spirit. 'The wind blows wherever it wishes.'[22] 'Now the Lord is Spirit, and where the Spirit of the Lord is present, there is freedom.'[23]

Oh Free Spirit, may your Wind blow through me. May my heart be filled with the Freedom of the Lord.

6 March (The Lord's Day)

One major theme prevailed in my sermons today: the nature of the Church and the difference between the Church and the World.

There are two major errors which are possible for the Church of Christ. One is conforming to this world. This is the common sin: the tragic Apostasy, the great Failure. Accepting the standards and values of the world and demeaning Christ and mutilating his Gospel to serve wickedness and corruption – this is the sin in which every member of Jesus Christ's Church participates.

The other error comes when Christians perceive that the Church has come to resemble the World and try to make the Church different from the World by imposing some constricting rules – ritual or moral rules – on Church members. How often Christians emphasize externals, rituals, creeds and prohibitions, to make their lives different from the life of the World. But that is the way of enslavement, not the way of freedom.

'Christ has set us free! Stand, then, as free people, and do not allow yourselves to become slaves again.'[24]

7 March (Monday)
Many Christians enjoy blaming the 'Church', and this could be an excuse for not searching into their own faults.

I am disgusted with myself today. I attempted to follow a meditation on Jesus' Temptation; I tried to face the deceits of evil within. But I completely failed to experience his nearness. I felt that Jesus was far away, and I was wandering in the desert. At last I made an effort to forget the disgust by reading various journals. But I did not succeed in escaping from it; the consciousness of the desolation of the desert was with me throughout the day.

Is not the life of *Homo sapiens* in the twentieth century a desert?

8 March (Tuesday)
The only hope for *Homo sapiens* is the foolishness of God.

'Ubi sapiens?... Nonne stultam fecit Deus sapientiam huius mundi!'[25]

My feeling today is that I am in the pit of despair.

The sin of the earth is like a burden upon me.

I feel that the Divine Potter cannot but tire of the earth. Does the earth not reject the guidance of the blameless Hands?

9 March (Wednesday)

Although a fit of despair for the earth came over me, my consciousness of God is livelier somehow: not the consciousness of the presence of the Creator and Comforter who has been a regular part of my experience during recent years, but a terrifying consciousness of the power and sovereignty of God.

Scientists in this atomic age are playing with the stuff of creation. Their ignorance is not much less than mine, and they cannot guarantee that this globe will not explode and melt as a result of some atomic experiment. Is this not another way of saying that the Potter can throw the intractable vessel to the floor?

It is no wonder that existentialists like Sartre and Heidegger talk of man's life as some kind of speck of will and energy strung in an unimaginable and comfortless emptiness.

The Potter, be merciful to the vessel, and pity me. It is on you that we totally depend. One movement of your Hand can destroy the world for ever. Save us, keep us. Through Christ the Lord. Amen.

10 March (Thursday)

I gained comfort from meditating on hymns and poems which talk of the Providence of God. Cynan's[26] long poem, 'The Lonely Isle' (about Father Damien's island), has proved helpful to me in the past, and it is still helpful to me. The trouble on the island was not without purpose prior to Damien's sacrifice.

Neither was God's work in calling this planet into being purposeless. There is some truth in the fancies of Hiraethog:

When the roll call of the names of the stars
    Was called in the morning,
They all came singing and dancing
    Past the white throne:
In its turn, amongst the myriads,

Appeared our earth,
Divine Love blushed
When he saw it.

Wisdom pointed her finger at it;
She told Mercy
That is the chosen province,
The province of your inheritance;
Mercy's kindly eyes
Shot love after it,
And she has never withdrawn
That look back.

Yes, love is the touch of the Heavenly Hands, not whim.

11 March (Friday)

I experienced an hour of peace last night after writing in my dairy, and the consciousness of God the Father returned. Dante is correct. It is love that moves the stars. The love of God is like a warm blanket comforting my soul today.

> *Oh Lord of all serenity, give me the confidence that this world, despite every corruption, will glorify Your name; that the Church of Christ, despite every apostasy, will declare Your love throughout the earth; that my own soul, despite every disappointment, will be able to lean on your mercy for ever. Amen.*

12 March (Saturday)

Reading some of the hymns of Martin Luther and Paul Gerhardt was a profound experience. It is impossible not to perceive the difference between the two.

Luther is powerful, and occasionally bellicose (although he strikes a tender note as when he talks of the baby Jesus). 'Ein Feste Burg ist unser Gott'[27] is a trumpet of a hymn, and it is a pity that it is not sung more often in Wales. But it expresses the strength of the worshipper, the strength of trust in God: there is no self-sufficiency in it. By submitting himself before God, as in the hymn 'Aus tiefer Not schrei ich zu dir',[28] Luther had

57

strength to face the greatest dangers. It is the articles of faith that he usually provides.

In Paul Gerhardt there is a feminine element as compared with Luther's masculinity. There is passion and warmth in his attachment to Jesus, and charm and exceptional beauty in praise of nature's treasurers. I feel that there is something obnoxious in his most famous hymn, 'O Haupt voll Blut und Wunden',[29] a hymn which gave a boost to the theology of Blood and Wounds, but there is strength and courage and faith in his best hymns, like 'Ist Gott für mich, so trete'[30]; and there is an inspired beauty in his more well-known nature hymn, 'Gott aus, mein Herz, und suche Freud'.[31]

Gerhardt[32] rejoices in the beauties of the visible world and sees in them a mirror of the blessed beauties of the unseen heaven. There is wisdom in this. It is sinful to deny the beauty of the earth to enhance the beauty of heaven, and it is sinful to deny the glory of eternal abodes to honour the splendour of the earthly sea and mountain. God owns them all.

13 March (The Lord's Day)

Tonight I preached about Heaven, the eternal life in the company of God. Not a prize to be received on the other side of Jordan, but a blessing to be enjoyed now, and not only enjoyed but shared and spread abroad until the earth is full of it.

14 March (Monday)

Self-discipline, devotion, complete dedication to the work of the Lord – that is what is expected of the person who belongs to Jesus Christ. I know that it is the inner compulsions that matter, and I have been examining these, and I intend examining them again. But the outward details must also be considered – eating, and sleeping, and respecting the body for the Glory of the Creator.

Too much attention has been given to these details by Christian moralists – for two reasons. One is that the outward aspects of the dedicated life are easier to perceive than the inner glories; kneeling in prayer through the night is sufficient proof of a dedicated commitment for many religious people, but it is impossible to measure the height and depth of the Divine Love in the heart of a man, who may, perhaps, secretly worship his God by undertaking his daily tasks. Another reason is that the externals of life are important not only to the saint but to the worldly man, and Christians who have accepted the values of the world often place great emphasis on thrift and diligence, on early rising and eating moderately, even when they reject the central message of the Sermon on the Mount.

Jesus' greatest command is Love. It is preferable to break all the rules of respectability and getting-on-in-the-world than to break that command. And it is better to pray in a bed than to kneel prayerless in front of a picture of a crucifix.

But I must also consider the externals, in case I excuse anything that could be a hindrance to my service.

15 March (Tuesday)

My intention today, in this diary, was to note briefly some of the facts of my outward life but I must rather mention my meditation. I tried to be with the Saviour on the pinnacle of the Temple. He was standing with his eyes closed. Although I saw him, in my imagination, so close to me, he was yet far from me. I looked down and saw the faces of many people. Although they said nothing, I knew they were expecting a miracle, desiring to see some outward sign of God at work.

I was looking down and seeing a firmament of faces, myriads of people, expectant faces, superstitious faces, bored faces, disbelieving faces. Inert humanity which stretched out in front of me like a bog of corruption. And yet there was in me some longing to save them. I stretched my arms down to them. But some giddiness came over me.

I felt Jesus' arm around my back, and I believe that I saw his smile before the experience disappeared fairly swiftly.

Oh Lord Jesus Christ, keep me from falling. I am no better than my own people; I am no better than my enemies. Keep me from falling, for you are stronger than me.

16 March (Wednesday)

I don't sleep too much. Indeed, by today, I have developed the gift of living with less sleep than most people that I know. I can study more freely at night than in the morning, and my tendency when I was younger was to work until the early hours and to sleep on after it was time to rise. By now, I have learnt the art of burning the candle at both ends, although the morning's end is a little more difficult to light than the other. But one has to rise. The children must go to school and my beloved enjoys her daily work much more if she has a cup of tea in bed. *Laborare est orare.*[33] I find it disagreeable to stay in bed too long.

It is another matter whether I use all my time and all my energy as I should. I do not read for entertainment, although I am entertained when I read. I spend only a little time reading the newspaper and novels. I know of industrious ministers who manage to find time to become experts on detective novels. I don't have time to read unnecessary books nor to listen to unnecessary readings. I do not visit the cinema except on those rare occasions when films are shown which are worth seeing, and not always then... There is no time either to be much interested in sport. I do not wish to boast of my busyness: one could argue that life is incomplete without some indispensable recreation.

But my lack of knowledge of films and sport is not on my conscience. My conscience is troubled rather by the paucity of time I give my family.

Some preachers talk of 'giving time to God'. But I learned that work and prayer were one. I am grateful for the Practice of the Presence of God.

Anna and Taranwen went out together tonight, and I gave the evening to the children. After playing a little with Ap

Siencyn and putting him to bed, I went through the book 'Lovely Things' with Flanagan. McTavish wanted me to tell a story but not from a book. For some reason I gave him the story of Romeo and Juliet. He laughed whole-heartedly but derisively at the foolish lovers.

17 March (Thursday)

I had a day of consultation and discussion, of proposing and seconding, of supporting and warning. But the Christ was with me, like a song in my heart.

18 March (Friday)

Old friends visited us, friends who had been estranged by circumstances to some extent. It was pleasant to feel all strangeness melting away in a moment of conversation.

19 March (Saturday)

Is it possible to trace the Gorsedd Prayer[34] back to its origins?

I am sure that the phrase 'Give, God, Your Protection...' Protection, Power, Knowing, Knowing the Righteous, Loving the Righteous, Loving every Essence, Loving God... It is not sufficient to explain this by mentioning the deism and the nature religion of the eighteenth century. Whatever the date of the prayer it represents a kind of mysticism which is primal in Wales. It is a pity that our scholars have avoided the important subject of the Wisdom of the Ancient Welsh.

20 March (The Lord's Day)

I preached about Christian realism, the only faith which can look in the eye of Evil without being defeated.

I had a lengthy conversation with Maredudd. It is surprising how optimistic he is. Christianity, the Ecumenical Movement, Congregationalism, Wales and the Welsh language – he will not allow himself to be overcome by dejection. Neither is he foolishly opinionated either. But he is satisfied in doing his work for his causes without complaint and without disappointment. His life is marked by true wisdom.

CHAPTER 5

FLESH AND SPIRIT

21 March (Monday)

I had to travel far today. On the way I read a number of hymns from a German hymn book. It was intriguing to note the particular interest shown in Eternity among some of the hymn writers of the seventeenth century. The contemporary scene was so odious and so frightening that many gentle souls turned toward the Unchangeable. But how sad it is that they cannot see any way of serving Christ except by subjugating the passions, suppressing 'des Fleisches Luste'[1] as Johann Heermann says. The mildew of negativity covers much of our Christian piety.

22 March (Tuesday)

The words I wrote yesterday do not excuse me from surveying my carnal failures. I have been reading the ancient history of Saint Pelagia and Saint Nonnus: Nonnus, unlike the other ascetics, acknowledges the magnificence and beauty of the famous prostitute, and she, by giving consideration to Nonnus, acknowledges the higher magnificence of his beauty, the beauty of holiness. The story blesses the work of Pelagia[2] after her conversion, when she destroyed her own attractiveness through fasting. God does not desire this: we must consider every earthly beauty as part of the means of grace which was given to us to lead us to the Eternal Beauty. But the flesh must be sanctified to make it a good companion for the spirit.

'The Word was made flesh and dwelt among us.'[3] That is the whole magnificence of the flesh.

In what sense and to what degree is fasting part of Christian devotion? The extreme and ascetic fasting which received so much praise amongst the early monks and their admirers must be condemned. Condemnation must also be levelled at the formal and easy and mechanical and ceremonial fasting which is part of the discipline imposed by hierarchical church bodies on their faithful. These things are contrary to the freedom and joy of Jesus. For him life is a feast. Room is given by him to fasting only as a help to the prayerful life: not as something to draw the attention of men but as a help to deep meditation at particular times. Usually a life of service to God demands that we eat enough to support us healthily in our work, and the greatest virtue here is moderation, which means accepting and using and sharing all the gifts of God to the glory of the Giver.

Jesus' fast in the desert during the Temptation was an inevitable part of that special meditation and was an expression of sympathy with ordinary people in their need. When lack of work was a nightmare for many Welsh people before the last war a number of patriots used to miss one meal a week and give it to the unemployed.

This is an example of fasting which is a challenge to us.

I must confess before God that I have neglected fasting as an act that can in special circumstances give intensity to loving prayer. I must also confess that I do not always eat and drink with the thankfulness and the Christ-like awareness which makes every meal a sacrament.

Oh Father God, fill my life with thanks and praise. Let me accept your gifts joyfully and use them obediently. Make my body a temple for the Holy Spirit. Amen.

I enjoyed a chat tonight with a young minister. The topic was the ministry. Before long many Christian causes will cease to be because of a shortage of ministers and a shortage of public leaders and supplicants in prayer. It has been a mistake to concentrate all the gifts of the ministry in the minister and to fail to realize that the gifts of the Spirit were given to the whole Church.

23 March (Wednesday):

I feel ashamed when I think of the passionate devotion of the Christian ascetics – 'God's athletes'[4] as they were once called. I disagree completely with their basic belief, that is, in the words of one of them, 'I am killing my body because my body is killing me.' I know that God owns the body as well as the spirit. Hatred for the body originates from the ancient dualism which gave birth to Gnosticism and Manichaeism. It is unhealthy. But I long for the same sacrificial passion which drove Christian zealots to face the loneliness of the desert and the hardship of fasting and hard work and vigils.

Once more I went with Jesus into the desert and I tried in my meditation to think with him. I held his arms and searched the depths of his brown eyes. 'Great Jesus,' I said, 'I know that you are God's will for me.' And in the eyes I saw nothing but Infinite Love, the Utmost Mercy. He was preparing himself for his saving work but he was not seeking the perfection of his own soul. It was the need of man that filled his heart. Bread in the desert, a miracle in the Temple, victory over the world; the support of life, the power of God, the salvation of mankind – these gave intensity to his appearance.

Oh the passion of those eyes! As I looked on them, I despised my own corruption. A voice rose from my heart: 'Jesus, save me.' And although the experience passed, I feel, as I write these words, the touch of Jesus' hands on my hands.

24 March (Thursday)

Since I returned home yesterday, life has been full of small troubles, and there was one great worry, the ill-health of a dear neighbour. Taranwen is with her now, trying to comfort her.

How painful is the suffering of one person; and in the world there are millions of sufferers.

My God, my God, Your Heart alone is big enough to suffer all the suffering that the whole earth suffers; but give me a heart which will be in accord with Your Heart. Give me a heart like Christ's heart, so that I can suffer with him and with You.

25 March (Friday)

I shall cleave quietly to your feet,
I shall sing of the virtues of the Blood;
I shall carry the Cross, I shall swim the wave,
Only if I have your nature beneath my breast.[5]

26 March (Saturday)

Here I am today meditating on care for the body as part of man's service to God.

Mortification of the flesh is the aim of the ascetic tradition, and very often this duty has been interpreted in a repugnant and insane manner. For example, observing the cleanliness of the body was not an aim at all for the early Christian ascetics. On the contrary, cleansing the body was a sign of spiritual weakness. In the sight of these strange champions there was virtue in dirt, and it would have been a heresy to claim that cleanliness was next to godliness. A stinking and flea-ridden body excelled over a clean body as the habitat for a pure soul. There is no more delectable story than the one about a famous saint who refused to clean his body and caused, by this, many dirty sores to appear on his skin. Worms crawled in the festering sores, and when at one time, one fell to the ground, the saint picked it up and put it back in the wound, saying 'Take the life which God has given you.'

God save us from such mortification. The body must be respected – and so must teeth and nose be respected, and nails and bowels be respected – and respect shown to water and soap and clean air. I have been a sinner many a time even in

65

these matters. Nurturing good practices and following them demands a considerable amount of discipline. I struggle and admit to an occasional failure even now. But God save us not only from an unhealthy and blasphemous mortification, but also from seeking cleanliness and bodily health before the cleanliness and salvation of the soul.

27 March (The Lord's Day)

In a part of a sermon this evening I spoke of the characteristics of a man who dedicated himself with a devoted heart to serve his God. I feel dejected when I think of how inadequate I am in zeal and commitment and loyalty to the truth. I cannot but think of Jesus looking at Peter after he had denied him. I had a glimpse of Jesus' face. Every self-righteousness was shattered by the pity on the face of my Great Friend.

28 March (Monday)

Here I am in a foreign city, in a meeting of numerous Christian committee men. This is not a place to escape from the world. Here, as in the world, there is some vying for office and influence, a certain amount of contention between party and party, a certain amount of concealing motives and falsely colouring intentions, a certain amount of shoddy flattery and of principled envy.

There is no escaping hatred and betrayal even among the 'saints'. I feel as if I'm caught in a net, and I do not know how to free myself from it.

But this also is an old story. It is impossible to read even the Book of Acts without seeing that conspiracy and ambition and partisanship pollute the Church early in her history.

Oh Lord Christ, in whom all the goodness of God and all the hope of man's life were concentrated, forgive us every untruth and every corruption. Forgive us by possessing us. Fill us with your Spirit. Live in us. Amen.

29 March (Tuesday)

I have no appetite for financial accounts, and when my fellow saints were discussing a balance sheet and funds and interest, my mind was this afternoon, once more, considering the great topic of Christian Commitment. Earlier I have been thinking about sleep and food and cleanliness. Today I turn in another direction: sex.

One idea which has caused great harm to the Christian tradition must be rejected completely, the idea that conception and birth are corrupt acts and that the *damnosa haereditas*[6] which is called sin and guilt is transferred from generation to generation in the sexual love which ensures the reproduction of life. On the contrary, sexual love is part of God's beneficent purpose. So God created human beings, making them to be like himself. He created them male and female, blessed them and said, 'Have many children so that your descendants will live all over the earth...'.[7] See how the Creator shares his creative energy with his creatures: there is a blessed connection between man's sexual nature and the *Imago Dei*. And I must testify in this diary that there is a glorious truth here which is part of my own experience. The closest intercourse between a man and a woman is full of sacramental enchantment; nothing shows more clearly the full glory of life, and in the height of rejoicing there is the marriage of earth and heaven, flesh and spirit, nature and grace.

But there is no more striking example than sexual love to show that *corruptio optimi pessima*, that the corruption of the best is the worst. Violence, madness, jealousy, degradation, torment, grovelling, self-glorification, defilement – all these occur when sex is corrupted. Even those who have avoided the more hideous corruptions have to accept that the sexual passions are unruly, and there are sexual incidents in everyone's history that we cannot mention even to our closest friends.

A means of grace, which mediates the joy of the morning stars – that is what the sexual passions are, on the one hand. On the other hand, this animated lust is a powerful and passionate impulse, an impulse which must be disciplined and tamed and led. It is very much like a brilliant, quick-footed stallion. What pleasure, what vigour it must be to ride on its back over the slopes in the wind, but the joy will only come to him who has learnt the art of horsemanship. Only the Author of Life can train us in the sciences of His Own Glory.

You are Life, my Lord, Life and Joy and Passion of all Creativity. Fill your servant with the light of Your heaven, fill my body and soul, my blood and imagination, fill my life with Your Life. Cause me to be enlivened and to rest in the flood of Your creative and reconciling Strength, and in the Love which is from eternity to eternity.

30 March (Wednesday)

Today I visited a magnificent cathedral, a Norman building with its internal arches of Caen stone rising on each other's shoulders in wing-like praise. Looking is synonymous with worship in a house such as this. The whole was craftsmanship to be enjoyed in sweet enchantment – thanks be to the Heavenly Architect.

How different was the meeting house I visited yesterday, the meeting house of the Lord, and the open Word in the centre before the eyes of the worshippers.

This is the difference between a skilful epic poem and plain prose. We can delight in the excellence of an *awdl*[8] but we are also grateful for the daily prose on which we are completely reliant.

31 March (Thursday)

I arrived home thoroughly exhausted, and heard good news and bad news.

Oh Father God, the Loving Paterfamilias, soothe the wretched of the earth – the frail, the weak, the fearful, the lost. Unite us in Your Own

Love. Through Jesus, the carpenter, the son of Mary, the brother of James and Joseph, Judas, and Simon and their dear sisters. Amen.

1 April (Friday)

A friend visited me, one of the special people, a man astute of mind and clean of spirit, who told me that he was certain that I was the Brother of Low Degree.[9] I grinned like an April Fool and admitted my guilt. Thank you my friend, for your astuteness and generosity and mercy.

2 April (Saturday)

My meditation returned again to the Temptation of Jesus. This was the subject of my first attempt to preach. Like Milton in *Paradise Lost* and Dostoevsky in the story of the Chief Inquisitor I feel that this is the heart of the life and work of Jesus. Neither the Incarnation nor the Atonement can be understood apart from the Will of Christ which declares the Divine Goodness and rejects all evil. The oftener the mind returns to the history of the Temptation, the greater the significance and the challenge.

The order of the temptations is different in Matthew to that in Luke. In the former Gospel the 'material' temptation (the stones) is followed by the 'spiritual' temptation (the pinnacle of the temple), and then, as a climax, there comes the contest between Christ and the Enemy for mastery over the kingdoms of the earth. In the other Gospel, the 'spiritual' temptation is the climax, the cunning temptation; and the Opponent, as it were, playing his last card. Perhaps this is the more solemn explanation, for the temptation to throw himself from the pinnacle of the temple is a kind of parody of the Sacrifice of the Cross itself. If this order is accepted the three temptations must be classified as follows: the economic temptation amongst the stones of the desert, the political temptation on the high mountain top, and the religious temptation on the pinnacle of the temple.

I tried to think of Jesus on the pinnacle, and I found myself as a member of a great crowd which was looking at him expectantly and shouting at him. In my heart there was a great longing for the conversion of the world, for an outpouring of the Saving Power on the children of men, for something which could convince every heart and every conscience that Christ and his love are the only Way. But despite the loud shouting, I heard a whisper from somewhere: 'If you are the son of God, throw yourself down.'[10] But Jesus stood firm in his place.

On thinking about Jesus the second time I saw him, not on the pinnacle of the temple, but on the Cross, and I, as before, one of a number of people staring at him. How lonely and how brave he was. And I heard as from the past the rebuke: 'Save yourself and come down off the Cross.'[11] But the Crucified stayed on his Cross.

Jesus never attempted to convince people through outward signs. The only sign of his Deity is his Love, and his beneficent works are 'signs' of his Love.

It is through this Love that the world will be convinced. 'That they all may be one, Father; just as you are in me and I am in you. May they be one, so that the world believes that you sent me.'[12]

3 April (The Lord's Day)
Oh that I could be worthy of the Crucified whom I preach.

4 April (Monday)
The mountains of our Lord's life: The Mount of the Sermon, The Mount of the Transfiguration, The Mount of Crucifixion, The Mount of Instruction, The Mount of Sonship, The Mount of Salvation – and The Mount of Olives as well, and the Mount of Temptation – I must preach on these one day.

I must stand with Jesus on the Mount of Temptation before I can stand with him on the other mountains. And yet seeing him on the other mountains brings me strength to conquer the evil in my own soul.

Seeing all the kingdoms of the earth and their glory and hearing the whisper, 'I will give you all this power and all this wealth. It has all been handed over to me, and I can give to anyone I choose. All this will be yours, then, if you worship me'[13] – that is a temptation I will have to face with Jesus. To gain supremacy over the world, according to the Tempter, one must accept the methods of the world, conform to the world, worship the Power that rules the world. But it is all a lie. Every supremacy that is not of God is vain and fleeting, and the claim that it is to the Evil One that the power and the glory has been given on this earth is vain and fleeting – although a number of astute theologians have swallowed this second part of this Gospel according to Satan.

There is only one answer: 'Worship the Lord your God and worship only him.'[14]

5 April (Tuesday)

One *vade mecum* which I carry with me everywhere is *Emynau'r Eglwys*[15] which was a gift distributed by Undeb Cymru Fydd to the Welsh men and women who were abroad in the armed forces in the last war. There is suffcient in the book to lift us to heaven – and without doubt there is enough to abolish the armed forces for ever.

It gives intense pleasure to go through the book and remember Jesus on the Cross.

Oh noble Jesus, who except you
Could die for us,
And take us from disgrace to eternal honour?
Who can ever forget this.

The Blood that ran on the Cross
Is remembered from age to age;
The expanse of eternity is too short
To speak properly of him.

The earth and its treasures will be burnt,
But the words of my God will stay the same;
Eternal life is to know my Saviour
As God and as man.

I shall abide quietly at your feet,
I shall sing of the virtues of the blood,
I shall carry the cross, I shall swim the wave,
Only if I have your nature beneath my breast.[16]

CHAPTER 6

DEATH AND RESURRECTION

6 April (Wednesday)

It is impossible for me to write in my diary today. I saw great weakness and frailty in the face of one dear to me and I have been in the presence of a friend's anxiety and sorrow.

Our lives are battle grounds. The Dark Death, the Great Executioner, the General-in-chief of the cohorts of Hell, who can raise his terrible banner over every human body and parade with terrifying pride over every member. But the Christ will reign.

> *Oh Lord Christ, the Resurrection and the Life, the First-born from the dead, take this precious life into your breast. Jesus, who wept in the past, accept our tears as a witness to the strength of Eternal Love who insists on calling his dear ones out of the grasp of the dust. Consecrate our grief to the glory of the Name which is above every name.*

7 April (Thursday)

The grief of the friend who is left is bitter. But the fierce anguish of the rent testifies to the strength of the partnership. The life together was not in vain: it is part of the Life together which is to eternity.

Does not the cry 'My God, My God, why have you deserted me?' convince us that God never leaves us?[1]

8 April (Friday)

*Oh Lord Jesus, King of the Jews, King of kings, King of the world,
accept our homage; for in You there is every virtue and every praise.
Your Cross is part of the fabric of the whole world, part of the pattern
of man's history, part of the witness of our conscience – the part
which gives meaning and light to the whole.*

*We have been one in sin; we are one in untruth. But this is the
oneness of hell, the deadly oneness which divides us against one
another and against our selves! Deliver us from evil. Unite us in your
Own Love.*

*We can see the false unity in the contempt of those who were
passing by and saying: 'Save yourself and come down from the cross';
in the words of the chief priest, 'He saved others but he cannot save
himself. Let us see the Messiah, the king of Israel, come down from
the cross now, and we will believe in him'; in the blasphemy of the
wrongdoer who was crucified with You, 'If you are the Messiah, save
yourself and us'; in the mockery of the soldiers, 'If you are the King
of the Jews, save yourself.'[2] We see the divided humanity uniting to
insult Your Love!*

*But you are interceding for us on the Cross. Oh the wonder of the
universe, unite us for ever in the endless forgiveness which glorifies
heaven and earth.*

*Comfort all the Companions of the Cross this day. The needy, the
sorrowful, the widow, the orphan, the one without hope and the one
without succour – take us all. You who were lifted from the earth,
draw us to Yourself. To whom shall we go but to You?*

9 April (Easter Eve)

I tried to accompany the Crucified One to the darkness of the
grave.

There seems to be a cold shiver in the word *claddu* (to bury).
There is something final, something terminal, associated
with this word. When I read Barth's first commentary on
the Apostles' Creed that is one of the things that struck me
most, the emphasis on the word *sepultus*.[3] Jesus was not only
crucified but buried – kept in the dungeon of the past.

But the great line by Ann Griffiths,[4] 'burying the stupendous

Resurrection', sends all the threatening shadows of the grave to flight and mocks the old Enemy.

In meditation I crawled into the grave and I felt the fog like a blanket around me. I sensed the deep darkness and the terror of it gripped my heart. And with darkness there was increasing silence. Gradually the silence became oppressive and agonizing until my soul was turned into a dumb scream for conversation and song and laughter. Deliverance did not come. For a few minutes I did nothing but listen intently to the empty silence of the black nothingness. But by listening I came to hear with increasing clarity the beats of Heart, the Cordium Choir, and the rhythm pounding within me like a hammer. And gradually the darkness became light. Not that light shone from the outside, but that the body of darkness itself shone like a new dawn.

I saw that darkness was as crucial as light – it was darkness that heard the command, 'Let there be light',[5] the darkness in the depths of the sea, the darkness of the soil, the darkness of the womb.

I became conscious of powers in the bright darkness. Life walked tremblingly over my lips, in my throat and along my spine. Life, pain, memory; thinking, experiencing, knowing; faith, hope, love – in all I felt that some sun was shining within me. Suddenly I was aware of myriads of arms stretching towards heaven, bare, entreating, longing arms, and the wonderful whiteness of the dawn on them.

'Unless a grain of wheat falls to the ground, and dies, it remains alone: but if it dies, it produces many grains.'[6]

10 April (Easter Day)

'And the colliery was no more.'

When I was a boy, seeing my father going to the colliery was like seeing the sun go down. I hated thinking of him descending into the darkness. I could see cruel fear on his face many times in the years between his two serious accidents. His last accident, although it was so hateful, was a release for him since it saved him from going down the pit ever again. I am certain that there is no colliery in his heaven. 'And the colliery was no more.'

I saw him after that, following years of pain and debility and the effort to live, falling into his grave, into the fog and silence of the soil.

When I think of the risen Jesus I cannot but think of my father, and his small body full of light.

I preached today on the grain of wheat.

'Oh fool, when you sow a seed, it does not sprout to life unless it dies. And what you sow is a bare seed, perhaps a grain of wheat or some other grain, not the full-bodied plant that will later grow up. God provides that seed with the body he wishes; he gives each seed its own proper body.'[7]

11 April (Easter Monday)

Sorrow, longing, heartbreak – I have seen these in the faces of dear ones. At times I have cursed Death, but I also had a glimpse of the Blessing which overcomes every curse.

'When the body is buried, it is mortal; when raised it will be immortal. When buried, it is ugly and weak; when raised it will be beautiful and strong. When buried, it is a physical body; when raised it will be a spiritual body.'[8]

12 April (Tuesday)

Let God's Israel always remember
That the Lamb who was slain is still alive![9]

I have been looking over some of the hymns on resurrection and victory and the ascension of Christ.

It is not the empty tomb which gives a convincing testimony for the resurrection, but rather the heavenly vision which Paul received on the road to Damascus: seeing, experiencing, knowing Jesus.

In these days spring is leaping upon us like a young animal.

The loveliness and gentleness of the beautiful primroses, the elegant courage of the daffodils, the common drollery of the daisy – there is no flower more Welsh than the daisy – and the trees and bushes expressing their strength and freshness and the godly sun challenging the mastery of the cold wind – it is such a privilege to be able to live on the earth. The lambs are growing – and the Lamb of God is ever on the altar of the universe. And the Lamb who was killed is still alive.

13 April (Wednesday)

I went to the Garden of the Resurrection with Mary Magdalene. This prodigal Mary smiles on me occasionally from the pages of the Gospels. In her rich tresses and her shapely breasts and her eyes which can dance like the sunlight on the Sea of Galilee I perceive all the vivacity and beauty of the flesh. I see traces of her folly on her as well. Hers is not the pale beauty of innocence. Her beauty is the beauty of one who expends her life and who was saved to a new life. Expend: the wonder of her spending is seen in her sanctity as well as her prostitution. She is a prodigal one. There is no meanness in her sin or in her goodness. Give, spend, waste – that is her gift. But as I draw near to her I feel that the glory of the ointment of valuable pure nard has kissed away all the aromas of her past, and in her hand she carries perfume with which to anoint him.

She is searching for the body, blind with tears. But on hearing the voice calling her name she turns to her Lord, and sees his glory through her tears. And she is the first who will see and recognize the First-born from the dead.

Oh Loveable Jesus, do not turn from me. I need to see and recognize you. Many times you have been with me, touching me, smiling on me, laughing gently at my bungling life. But now I want to see you and the light of the White Throne on your sacred wounds. Do not turn away from me, Glorious Jesus. Let me embrace you, You Comeliness of heaven and earth. In you is noon and night, autumn

and spring, the wrench of death and the jubilee of heaven, the hope of
man and the sublimity of God. Do not turn away from me. Stay with
me. You, my Lord and God, are the Eternal Life.

14 April (Thursday)

There is nothing as beautiful as a lonely star above the horizon
when night is approaching but without the sky yet darkening.

As I look at it I know it was God who warmed my heart.
There is strength, stability, assurance in it. Yes, and in Christ,
as the old saints used to say, God has warmed the grave for
me.

Oh Exalted One, I belong to You.

15 April (Friday)

I contemplated the Body of Christ: the Body which touched the
sick, which moved from place to place doing good, and which
announced the acceptable year of the Lord, the Body which
was beaten and nailed on wood; the Body which rose from the
dead, which gave joy to Mary, which breathed a blessing on the
disciples, who came to the followers although the doors were
closed; the spiritual Body which stunned Paul and who came
so close to me, and the Body of which all those who love the
Gospel are members, that holy Church we are not worthy of
her, the Church which is more catholic than all the Catholics
and freer than all the Frees!

16 April (Saturday)

The Lord of the Resurrection is everywhere; in every live grain,
in every ball of fire, in all energy, in every empty space.

I had an opportunity today to look on an expansive scene.
Apart from the sea and the clouds and the sky there was no
beauty of nature in it; a big town and its factories and houses,
and beyond it, the grey sea and mist and cloud and the
immense gentleness of the sky; puny men with their narrow and
uncouth busyness, and around them the astonishing vastness

of the universe; chattering and complaining and smirking and snivelling and around everything the glory of the infinite mercy. And I felt that I was not worthy of the Christ who is in creation. Every movement, every breath, every crystal, every response to sun and shade – is this not the same power as in the Resurrection?

17 April (The Lord's Day)

Life overcomes Death because it is more alive. To suppose that Death can lord it over Life is synonymous to supposing that Non-being challenges Being.

The astonishing verse by Edward Jones, Maes-y-plwm, comes to mind. There is no more sublime verse in the literature of the world:

He fills the heavens, he fills the world,
He fills hell also;
He fills the infinity of eternity itself,
God is limitless;
He fills the empty space completely,
He is all-in-all, his power is one;
Infinite, illimitable Being,
And his essence is in Himself.[10]

Nothing could be more terrifying or more comforting.

And it came to me that there is no difference between Non-being and Essence but breath, the breath which creates, the breath which declares 'Let there be Light', and the breath which flares man's nostrils and comes to him from God.

I recently read for the third time the striking discussion by Vernon Lewis, in the last number of *Diwinyddiaeth*, of Non-existence, *Das Nichtige*.[11] A distinction must be made between Non-being and Non-existence.

The Non-being is completely harmless, the old non-creature: a little fool who is used by the Non-existent for his own purposes, some scarecrow who was placed in the Garden to frighten us.

One must wrestle with the Non-existent and his vicious retinue, the Tempter, the Accuser, the Enemy, the Blasphemer, the Father of Lies, the King of Filth, the Cancer of Creation, the Tyrant of the itches and the scabs and the corpses.

My sermons today all touched on the battle in our lives between the Giver and the Plunderer.

18 April (Monday)

Years ago I made a list of my favourite hymns in the *Caniedydd*.[12] It is interesting to look over it and to savour the hymns again. I expect that the list would be different if I were to make it today.

William Williams[13] is prominent in the list. My choice of hymns reflects my emphasis some years ago:

'I desire to see his beauty'

'Jesus, the pleasure of my precious heart'

'May my heart be a temple for you'

'Commencing to sing, commencing to praise'

'Christ and his shame'

'Oh converse with me, gentle Jesus'

'Ride, Jesus, with success'

'Unseen! I do love you'.

What riches there are in these hymns: a mystical union with Jesus; a passionate love towards him; a desire to be like him; the eternal glory of his sacrifice; the sufficiency of his work and blessing; the joy and authority of his words; the endless splendour of his victory; the magnificence of his incarnation and his company and his presence.

I received a blessing on meditating on these hymns, and Jesus came close to me – so gentle, so strong, so loveable – my Companion, my Friend, my Lord and my God.

The Glorious Invincible, may Your warm radiance shine on me for ever!

19 April (Tuesday)

The joy of the New Life and the sadness of the old sinful life weave together through and through in my heart as in the world. After every elevating experience, after every ecstatic rejoicing, I must face the corruption which is within me and around me:

> Draw my soul from its prison,
> Let the dawn now break;
> Smash in pieces the doors of Babel –
> Pull the iron bars free.[14]

20 April (Wednesday)

We went for a walk in the country this afternoon – and our friend's dog searching vainly for rabbits. The greenery is becoming wonderful now. We saw a crow chasing a hawk, flying after it and around it and stretching to peck it occasionally. The hawk did nothing except seek to escape. We watched the birds until they disappeared from our view. This was a strange turn.

Life is a mystery. The mystery cannot be explained except by its purpose. From age to age the Life of Creation has been struggling, seeking a new heaven and a new earth. Man was born to be closer to God than the beast. In Christ the closeness is a complete sonship.

To see the significance of the Christ one must wonder at him not only from the light but also from the mud.

21 April (Thursday)

I turned to the other hymns on the list I once made. The hymn by Dafydd William, 'Oh Lord give us a breeze',[15] is in it – a hymn totally distinctive of the author, and the repetition of the words 'breeze' and 'breezes' and 'Mount Sinai' are like importunate knocks on the door of heaven. There are two hymns by Morgan Rhys on the list – another great hymn writer – namely 'He opened a door for the captives' and 'Enlarge the boundaries of Your kingdom'. I also note four hymns by David Charles, 'Oh exalted Jesus, extend your pure nature' – so blessed – and 'We can ascend from the perplexing wilderness' and 'Oh that I could have a captivating glimpse' and 'The magnificent providence of heaven' – four wonderful hymns so different from one another.

Robert ap Gwilym Ddu is there once with his 'The blood which ran on the Cross', and Pedr Fardd twice, with 'I shall go from strength to strength' and 'Before the world was formed, before the heavens were spread'.

God's Purpose and Providence on the one hand, and the Eternal Wonder of the great Sacrifice on the other hand – I am doubtful whether there are in the literature of the world more passionate declarations of these themes as in the Welsh hymns. This is the lasting contribution of Calvinism, and in the poetry of our hymns the formal doctrines rejoice and flower like a rose.

There is a mixture of other hymns in the old list. 'Let Jesus' dear name be exalted' by Ieuan Glan Geirionydd; 'Speak, Lord, until everyone hears' by R J Derfel; 'Although my flesh is but straw' by Ehedydd Iâl; 'The pure rays of the dawn spread' by David Lewis; 'Look beyond the clouds of time' by Islwyn; 'Oh crucified Jesus' by Ieuan of Lleyn; 'Here is love like the oceans' by Hiraethog; 'Gospel of peace' by Eifion Wyn; 'See the day is dawning there' by John Thomas; 'You, great Creator of the heaven' by Ben Davies; and two by Elfed, 'The Lord holds me in mind' and 'A little baby in a manger was found'. I am rather surprised to see only one hymn by Ann Griffiths, 'How sweet it is to remember the Covenant'. How stupendous was her vision!

22 April (Friday)

> To put the Author of life to death
> To bury the massive Resurrection;
> To bring in eternal reconciliation
> Between the highest heaven and lowly earth.[16]

23 April (Saturday)

I still feel that I hide my sins from myself.

A wave of dejection came over me today: a feeling that the best experiences I had were unreal, even the most sacred experiences. Easter week and the previous week were periods of profound experiences, sad and joyous. But I find myself today failing to consider anything seriously. A spiritual *ennui* is upon me; somehow I fail to grasp anything, failing to believe even in my own recent experiences.

Everything is distant from me.

I do not know whether there is a connection between this feeling and my physical condition. I experienced two painful nights recently and I consulted the doctor. I had no worries after that, nor did I think of the pains – not consciously at any rate; but perhaps there is some anxiety lurking under the surface. I am also tired.

But the feeling of failure in me today has been cutting. When I think of the hopes of my youth I am troubled by disappointment; when I think of the idols of the age my heart is overwhelmed by abhorrence; when I think of the corrupt worldliness and the apathetic advance in the direction of war and destruction and the absence of any sympathy on the part of the society in which I live, I feel as if I'm drowning in a sea of helplessness.

24 April (The Lord's Day)

There was some discomfort and some mishap in every service today. I feel as if I have gone through the postures of preaching, having given a mediocre performance, after having weakly announced judgement and grace in statements which became platitudes on my lips.

I am tired of myself.

I had no feeling of the presence of God today, despite seeking it earnestly.

Lord, Lord, forgive me. Meeting house, the saints in their seats, the organ playing a hymn, lesson, hymn, prayer, hymn, sermon, hymn, blessing and I sit, a failure, and some vast desolation within me, with no word in me except some whisper of a curse on the day I was born – forgive me, oh my God. All the magnificence of the Gospel, all the wonder of the Holy Scripture, all the nobility of the great Church in heaven and earth, and me seeing the whole disappearing like a mirage – oh merciful Father, forgive me, save me.

There is poison in me.

25 April (Monday)

What grief it is to seek the Saviour and to find only the merciless Accuser. I have not yet dared to look on my more heinous sins. The awful silence of the Accuser shows that I am not yet pure.

'Blessed are the pure in heart; for they have seen God.'

26 April (Tuesday)

There is a desolation within me. There is emptiness around me. According to the hymns, Christ fills the void and turns emptiness into glory. Despite every abhorrence I know today that this is true:

His gift and grace and costly love
Fill the heavens, fill the world.

He grasped man on the ground,
He brought him and the Deity as one;
The distance between them was vast
He filled it with His own merit.

Jesus, the great fullness of heaven.

Where, and how can I begin
To praise the exalted Jesus?
I cannot track his grace –
He fills heaven and earth.

27 April (Wednesday)

I remember reading a scientific article recently about the astonishing empty spaces which are in the universe. In thinking about the Christ filling the far-off reaches and the empty spaces I turned to meditate about the strange vast spaces of the natural world. Eddington says that the number of stars in the universe is 10 to the power 22 (which is a million multiplied by a million multiplied by a million by ten thousand): my surprise is that anyone dares to put the number so low. Of course, much depends on the meaning given to the word 'universe'.

The emptiness of the universe is even more surprising than the number of stars. The stars of the universe do not take up more room that a few spots of dust in the big marquee at the National Eisteddfod.[17] And unlike the empty spaces in the large marquee at the Eisteddfod, the spaces in the universe are truly empty – as far as the scientists can say.

The same wonderful emptiness is in the strange world of the molecule and the atom. To find the number of molecules in a glass of water the stars of the universe must be multiplied sixty times. If it were possible to place this number of molecules in a straight line they would extend for a distance a thousand times more than the distance between the sun and the earth. But there are vast spaces of emptiness in every molecule and atom. In every part of 'matter', it is only six parts out of a hundred million which exist: all else is emptiness.

Natura abhorret a vacuo, according to the scientists in the past – 'Nature abhors a vacuum.' The opposite is true according to the teaching of scientists today. 'Nature enjoys a vacuum' – that is the truth now, although the other claim is still correct within limits.

No one can fully understand the claims above, the claims of scientists today, and no one can comprehend the numbers which I so innocently wrote. For this reason, the terror of the empty spaces preoccupies us only a little. The imagination fails in its attempt to comprehend the immensity.

After writing the above words I made an effort to test the empty spaces. In my imagination I sailed in a vague space ship and travelled the 'wide heavens': leaving Wales, Britain, Europe behind, slipping past the moon and onwards, and the Milky Way below me and above my head and around me; and moving spuriously in the midst of the innumerable fires of the stars until I felt that I was lost amidst a myriad of wonders. My imagination failed.

Who can live in this void?

I had a feeling as if my soul was fainting. Foolish questions entered my heart.

Is there Anyone living there? Is there Anyone responsible for this place? Where is the Caretaker, the Ruler, the Owner?

I returned to the words that I wrote on Tuesday:

Where, and how can I begin
To praise the exalted Jesus?
I cannot trace his grace –
He fills heaven and earth.

Oh God my Father and Saviour, convince me that Grace can save where Nature fails. You are the great Occupier, the Eternal House Owner. Protect my weakness now and for ever. Through Jesus Christ. Amen.

28 April (Thursday)

His gift and grace and costly love
Fill the heavens, fill the world.

29 April (Friday)

We must have a theology of the atom.

I saw the Christ hanging on the sky and his hands touching the extremities of the orbit.

'Oh Father forgive them.'

Oh Father, forgive me.

30 April (Saturday)

I saw a delectable part of the beauty of Wales this morning, and the splendour of sky and sea bringing the beauty so near. The gorse is like a fire smouldering on bank and slope. How futile are man's attempts to picture the world with brush and camera.

I have stood in wonder many times before art masterpieces, but the sentence is inevitable: 'but the half of it was not declared to me'.[18]

Indeed, dead pictures have ruined our appreciation of the beauty of nature. We fell into the habit of attempting to see nature 'still as in a picture' – some motionless, unnatural, dead moment pulled violently out of the ever-moving flood of life. We are in danger, when appreciating a view, of loosing sight of curve and wriggle, of effort and fall, of the varying oscillations of creation – of life itself and all its thrusting aspirations participating in the astounding venture of Creation.

Pinning a butterfly until it is dead on a board – the 'representative' artist cannot achieve this much. To present the dawn as a corpse in its blood, to present the sunset as a tin of salmon spilled on to a carpet – oh that the artist could achieve such a feat as this!

We rejoice in art – and we must beware of it coming between us and nature.

We can but collapse into indignation on hearing the sentence passed on my young fellow countryman Chris Rees.[19] May the Holy Warrior be close to him in his imprisonment.

It is a great encouragement to remember his, and others', courage in Wales.

While I prayed for him I found myself being envious of him. He has had the honour of suffering as a prisoner for Wales. I desired the honour many times. I fear that sin lurks even in that desire. Certainly I am not belittling the cruelty of the calamity: the heartless months trying to tear the soul.

1 May (The Lord's Day)

I received more of a blessing as I preached today. The merciful Jesus was at my side to strengthen me in my weakness.

I feel that I have not told him everything about my lies and failures, but I also feel that he knows everything and that he is willing to be easy on me.

2 May (Monday)

I meditated once more on the empty spaces of the universe. My spirit was struck as before by the wondrous hymn of Edward Jones, Maes-y-plwm, and I feel that I experienced his Omnipresence. In the fullness of his glory, God extends between star and star, between electron and electron, between soul and soul. It is He who rules, between sun and leaf, between precipice and tongue, between wing and crystal, between lament and resurrection:

> He fills the heavens, he fills the world,
> He fills hell also;
> He fills the infinity of eternity itself,
> God is limitless;
> He fills the empty spaces completely,
> He is all-in-all, his power is one;
> Infinite, illimitable Being,
> And his essence is in Himself.

He is in Swansea prison now, in every prison in the world.

Oh my gentle Lord, who was once a prisoner, may your love be known to all who are languishing within walls. Visit your brother and sister who are in captivity. Keep your faithful people bold. Make your home in every broken heart. For the sake of your Cross. Amen.

CHAPTER 7

CONFESSION

3 May (Tuesday)

I feel that I must face my sin more thoroughly before I can receive an increase in grace. I sometimes have the desire to confess my fault before men; but I have not yet confessed everything before God.

I got hold of an ancient form of confession which was used by Christians who would confess privately before a priest: 'I confess before God the Father Almighty and his Only Begotten Son Jesus Christ, and God the Holy Spirit, and all the host of heaven, and before you, also, my father, that I have committed these sins... I am truly sorry for these sins, and for others that I do not remember, and I am determined to improve my conduct immediately; I humbly ask for pardon from God; and of you, my spiritual father I beseech that I will suffer penance, and receive guidance and release. Therefore I pray God the Father Almighty, and his Only Begotten Son Jesus Christ and God the Holy Spirit to have mercy on me, and ask you my father to pray for me to the Lord our God. Amen.'

I fear that this formal prayer is completely hollow for me in my present condition. But confession is important – not the secret confession but the brotherly confession. 'So then, confess your sins to one another and pray for one another, so that you will be healed. The prayer of a good person has a powerful effect.'[1] That is one of the purposes of this diary: confession – acknowledging my fault before God and before my own soul and before my brothers and sisters in Christ. I expect that anyone who troubles to read these confessions will come to know who I am; and I hope that some of them pray for me.

4 May (Wednesday)

> Cover my faults from the people,
> Cover them from the righteousness of heaven;
> Remember the blood that once was shed
> On the cross in my stead.[2]

In these words William Williams is not asking for his faults to be covered in order to deceive, but to blot out evil by being amazed at the good. And to cover evil like this it must be revealed in the light of the Sacrifice.

> Let my passions, like musicians,
> All play with their fine fingers
> On the harp which resonates
> With Jesus' own magnificent name.

5 May (Thursday)

I have an old Anglo-Catholic book which contains a list of sins. It is a most varied list. 'Allowing our love towards someone else to interfere with our duty towards God. Allowing our love of the world, of pleasure, of money to gain control of our hearts... Putting my own judgement above the doctrine of the Church. Thinking that religion is a troublesome thing... Failing to admit my own faults... Curtailing my prayers because I fail to rise in time... Failing to give thanks after communion... Looking around the Church building... Going to places of worship without belonging to the Church... Repeating facetious stories from some scriptural history or subject... Being disrespectful of God's ministers... Transgressing on Feast Days by over-eating and excessive pleasure... Working, or occasioning others to work unnecessarily on the Sunday... Lacking respect for my elders... Harshly judging the wealthy or those who are superior to me... Wishing to die... Rejoicing in hearing about the misfortunes of others... Joining in unseemly talk. Reading the Bible from corrupt compulsions. Reading corrupt books, and corrupt stories in the newspapers... Gambling... Running into debt without any hope of paying... Avoiding taxes... Giving too small a wage... Elaborating on stories by repeating them... Reading other people's letters... Attempting to appear worse than I am...' There is plenty of room for argument on some of these.

6 May (Friday)

'You place our sins before you, our secret sins where you can see them.'[3]

7 May (Saturday)

Oh good God, Eternal Glorifier of the dust and mud, Father of the whole prodigal world, Brother and Saviour of sinners, Comforter of the prophet and the apostle and saint, the Great Reconciler, here I seek reconciliation with you. How often I have hated my sin and yet failed in the act, and hid my sin from my own eyes. My gracious God, give me the fullness of repentance. Dwell in my heart; establish Your Kingdom there; subdue my whole life with your holy powers; make me altogether Yours. Let me know You as you are and live every hour of my life in Your presence. Give me the ineffable sweetness as an abiding pleasure. And let me see the world as an abode for the Highest and my fellow men as brothers and sisters to the Saviour who made Cross and Throne as one. For the sake of the Name that is above every name. Amen.

8 May (The Lord's Day)

With some gusto, from time to time, I have attacked the worldliness and cowardice of the Church as she is in her corrupt, imperfect condition. But consciousness of my own sin was a hindrance to me today. And yet I was conscious of the

Presence, the Saviour and Accuser that were there, and they were one.

His chastisement is in His love.

9 May (Monday)

On looking back on my diary I see that I have mentioned mainly the sins of the flesh.

If there are degrees of sins, these, without doubt, are the lesser sins. I talked about work and the proper way to use time; about eating and sleeping; about care of the body; about the sexual life. The monks of the Middle Ages considered the failures and mistakes in these matters as examples of sins of the flesh – bodily laziness, apathy of soul, gluttony and luxury, lust and impurity. There are other sins, the sins of the world and the Devil.

On re-reading pieces of the diary, I fear that I have shown a degree of satisfaction with my own busyness. I forgot one thing: I am busy with the work which is interesting to me and in the work I must do. I burn both ends of the candle without complaint when there is enjoyment in the work. When the work is not to my taste I am not so uncomplaining, but I will do it if I have to. But I have an antipathy to thinking about work which I have neglected because it is uninteresting and because there was no essential necessity for me to do it.

I do not forget the languages which I have failed to learn. I dread to think of the wasted time that has been in my life. There has been vain effort after vain effort to learn languages, and failure has followed failure because of a lack of perseverance.

Is this a sin? (Is not every waste a sin?) Is it the flesh that is weak? (Is not every weakness a sin?)

*

Perhaps I am wasting time now by discussing the little sins – if, indeed, they are sins. But I am going to be honest.

I have not touched on the territory of King Tobacco. I do

smoke, and I give up smoking shamefully often. I am a moderate smoker – less than an ounce of tobacco a week sometimes, and an occasional cigarette. But, I wish that I had the money which I expend on smoke to buy new Welsh-language books.

I do not wish to be unbalanced. I have a great admiration for some dedicated Christians whose lives are as smoke-infested as hell, and it is possible to argue that they would be less dedicated if they rejected the comforting smoke. And surely, to believe that lighting a pipe or cigarette is a worse sin than making a hydrogen bomb is a much worse sin than to expire from smoking.

But since I am attempting to be perfectly honest, I intend putting even these things on the record. And I do not intend to confess all in detail.

You, Brother of Low Degree, are a creature of flesh and blood, weak, lazy, enslaved, totally lacking in control of taste and appetite, of feeling and instinct. Remember that, when you are tempted to think that you are stronger and busier and more self-controlled than others. I am a coalescence of primitive lusts, a verminous bag of animal cravings and of murky lusts.

There is only one comfort for you in your vomit and stink.

The word which was made flesh, and who dwelt in our midst.

Crucified One, in your unbearable blood and thirst, have mercy on me. Guide me. Sanctify me. Let my flesh partake of the glory of the Cross.

10 May (Tuesday)

There are two ways of imposing order on disorder: through fear or through love. The flesh can be tamed to some degree by putting it under an iron and oppressive compulsion. Or it can be induced and led and disciplined by setting an aim for it: the Christ, and the flame of his endless goodness attracting us and lighting our path.

Fear and love, oppression and understanding – that is the

choice. But the way of fear and oppression will fail in the end and the passions, imprisoned for so long, will explode and disperse destructively across the world.

11 May (Wednesday)

Little Flanagan is wholly shameless in her thoughtlessness when there is food she likes on the table. When her mother is rebuking McTavish for daring to ask for the third cake, Flanagan will craftily steal her fourth or fifth without asking anyone's permission.

The appetite for tasty food is healthy, of course. Wrongdoing is introduced when the rights of brother or sister to enjoy the same pleasure are ignored.

When I rebuked Flanagan I could not help remembering that I, even now, am not wholly free of the same fault.

But that is enough of my feeble honesty for today.

One of the funniest things in Tegla's satirical novelette, *Gyda'r Glannau*,[4] is the description of the young hero deciding to enter the ministry after noting that his mother had prepared a chicken for the preacher's supper.

Today, of course, many young men see more hope for a chicken supper in other occupations.

But I must cease. Who called this diary a spiritual diary?

12 May (Thursday)

I enjoy leafing through books that present a theory of evolution and trace the lineage of humanity back to the ape-man and the ape and four-footed creatures and the reptiles of the shores and the fish and the most primal forms of life in the sea and mud. The few books which I have on the subject are misleading by now since they give attention to the Piltdown Man who has now been proved to be a fake and a deceit. But the story, although it is uncertain in places, is extremely interesting, and gives new meaning to the Franciscan custom of calling his fellow creature a brother.

I am extremely similar to my brother the Frog: eyes, mouth,

legs; desire and taste; gobbling, moving, lying, procreating, dying, rotting.

And it was for my sake that Christ was raised to the Cross.

13 May (Friday)

Taranwen had her birthday today. It was a happy birthday, and Taranwen greatly enjoyed the little presents from the children and thanked me for planning them so perceptively. Time flies – but seeing the love in her eyes still renews my youth.

14 May (Saturday)

On looking at the penitential pieces in the prayers of Lancelot Andrews, his *Preces Privatae*, I am struck by the occasional eloquent entreaty – such as 'Look upon me with your eyes, the same with which you looked at Magdalen in the feast, at Peter in the courtyard, the robber on the cross, so that I can, with the robber, plead in humility "Remember me when you come as king", weep bitterly with Peter – and oh that my eyes were like a fountain of tears so that I could weep night and day – with Magdalen hearing you say, "Your sins are forgiven," and with her to love greatly because I have been forgiven many sins many times.' But very often the emotion is over-powered by the construction and the formal exaggeration. There are parts which are totally unprofitable; no benefit comes from declaring before God that the supplicant is '1, an unclean vermin; 2, a dead dog; 3, a rotten corpse.' There is no benefit either in analysing sin, such as the sins of the heart, and the words and the action; sins against God, against our neighbour, against our own bodies, conscious and unconscious sins, sins which are remembered and those which are forgotten; sins when sleeping and when awake. There is an old tradition to these, but there is a difference between true repentance and analysing sin.

In the end, there is only one sin: lovelessness.

15 May (The Lord's Day)

What a great privilege it is to preach the Love, to preach the Cross. During the evening service my soul was possessed by the passion of the Crucified and I felt that I was looking down on my congregation from the Cross itself. I was held, somehow, by Jesus: the Crucified in his frailty and his agony and his nakedness and his shame is stronger than me. The experience passed quickly – before I finished preaching – leaving fear and brokenness behind in my heart.

16 May (Monday)

On looking over some of my confessions in my diary I was surprised to note how sparing are my comments on the sexual life. I spoke much more of its glory than of its dangers and its corruptions, and indeed my words give the impression that I have tamed the monster, Sex, for ever. The gloriousness is certainly part of my experience: the vivacity, the wonder, the communion, being lord of the universe, being subdued under the sceptre of love. But I have never tamed the Tyrant. The only thing that I can claim is that I have through grace arrived at a kind of modus vivendi. The tension is with me daily – between the feeling that I can ride the universe and the terror of looking down on the inferno of my passions.

From time to time a story arrives of someone who has committed a sexual sin, a story about an adulterer or homosexual or rapist or exhibitionist, and the story will be the subject of gossip and clack. If a minister is the sinner, the commotion can be quite widespread. A minister is expected to be an exemplar, and this is appropriate and inevitable. It is not without reason that we say 'the revered, fearful vocation'.

I wonder whether William Williams, Pantycelyn, was thinking of his vocation after all (to some degree, at any rate) as he composed 'Cover my faults from the people'?

Nothing can show more clearly than this the distinctiveness of the ministry – and its glory also. But every time I hear of a sexual offender, be it a minister or not, I am compelled by my conscience to confess in my heart, and occasionally with my tongue, as John Bradford did, 'There but for the grace of God go I.'

I must acknowledge that most of the perversions that I hear about are present in my blood and imagination. There is a crowd in me, an unclean and innumerable crowd, a jungle of cravings. God only knows how fierce is the civil war that is fought within me. If there is one confession that I can claim as my own, it is that of the madman amongst the graves: 'My name is "Legion", since there are so many of us.'[5]

I give the impression to some that I am a passionless, placid, unfeeling man. How difficult it is to know one's fellow man. Sometimes I imagine that all the demons within me keep themselves in order, since they are all so numerous and so strong. Perhaps this is one aspect of the grace of God – keeping a balance of power between inclinations which could be totally destructive. But there is no relief until the whole personality is led and directed by the Great Master.

The Christ, the Supreme Superego, possess my flesh, possess my life and every life, be the Soul for the unruly Body of the universe.

There is no escape from Brother Ass. 'What an unhappy man I am! Who will rescue me from the body that is taking me to death?'[6] But the Christ can ride into Jerusalem on the back of the dear ass.

Neither de Sade or Sacher-Masoch can say anything new to me.[7] But the new life in Christ is wholly a new life.

17 May (Tuesday)
The Word was made flesh, ulcers, sweat.

18 May (Wednesday)
What a pearl of gentleness and courage is the *pericope adulterae* in the Gospel of John.[8] I saw them all as I meditated:

Pharisees and scribes cackling importantly and with empty authority, men uttering curses as they dragged the woman caught in adultery to Jesus' feet, and she screaming in fear and disappointment and shame. I saw Jesus writing on the ground.

'He knew what was in man.' Yes, the Word was made flesh.

I saw him writing with his finger on the earth, wrestling with humanity, while the self-important religious people kept multiplying words. 'He who is without sin, let him throw the first stone at her.'

He bowed again and wrote on the earth.

I saw their faces: the pride faded, the thick-lipped filth came into view, and the stink of the hidden lusts besmirched every self-satisfaction. I saw them looking at one another. Some knew one another quite well.

I saw an elderly man turn and move away with others following and lastly the young ones, and the heat of their own bodies testifying against them.

The woman was weeping quietly by now.

'Go and sin no more.'

One could not help hearing the authority in the gentle voice.

19 May (Thursday)

There is one place at least, in T Gwynn Jones' translation of Goethe's *Faust*,[9] where the translator improves greatly on the original. It is odd that there is not more quoting of Gwynn Jones' translation. For the German reader *Faust* is full of well-known quotations, and Gwynn Jones has put a shine on some of them. And this is one:

Fe greodd yn fy mynwes eirias gwyllt
A'm tynnu yn brysur at bob prydferth lun;
Felly y treiglaf o flys i flas,
Ac yn y blas, hiraethu am y blys.[10]

It is true of much of our lives: this is the misery of sin. But there is glory also, and in Christ the glory speaks distinctly.

20 May (Friday)

I have loitered enough for now with the sins of the flesh. The tireless Accuser is with me and the specific accusation is that I avoid looking at my worst sins. I must face the World and the Devil before perceiving my greatest sin.

Oh Lord Christ, I would give my body to be worthy of you.

21 May (Saturday)

The month of May has not dressed the thorn flowers as brilliantly as it did occasionally in the past, but I don't believe that I have noticed with such wonder the variety of the trees as they break into leaf. Graceful and playful, strong and patient, noble and sober, generous and worshipful – their beauty stands in meadow and hill – the faithful witnesses who tell us their story by growing and breaking into leaf and flowering and bearing fruit and waiting, waiting, waiting.

I would like to know what opinion the poplar has of the aspen, and the opinion the pine tree has of the silver birch. But their wisdom is deeper than our inquisitive and quarrelsome intellectualism. 'Judge not that you be not judged.' Live, and let live – the trees learnt this great art better than us.

'Make me as a tree planted, oh my God.'[11] I tried to imagine myself as a tree: growing and extending quietly, and the wind and rain and sun serving me. I raised my being towards the sun and acknowledged my total dependence on the Giver of Life; I gave thanks for the raindrops and for the abiding blessing of air; I stood firm under the buffeting of the storm and relished its strength and my strength. I experienced leaf growth, buds, flowers; I became aware of the rhythm of growth; the ebb and flow of the sap nearly overwhelmed and killed me. In the depth of winter I rejoiced in the nativity of the Unconquerable; the Glory rose to fill my life. I was able to live, to strive, to long.

The summer ruled in my branches and leaves. And then I was allowed to be part of the deadly dance of the autumn until I sank into the cold repose of winter.

But there. How poor are the liveliest imaginings. We can never know (except through a miracle that we cannot comprehend) what kind of rapture comes to a tree in spring and autumn.

22 May (The Lord's Day)

One of the greatest dangers to a preacher's soul is the flattery that is showered upon him. No one has to receive more of it than the preacher. The flattery starts in earnest on the day of his ordination, if it hasn't already done so. Some grow quite pompous under the treatment; others harden to such an extent as to be unable to respond to any word of praise. 'Truth through personality' is one of the best known definitions of preaching. God save us from being personalities that hide the truth.

23 May (Monday)

I enjoyed the journey to the Union.[12] The weather was so fine, and the countryside looked like a big stage with the exciting drama of the young summer being played upon it. The trees were the most obvious dramatis personae. I noticed once more, with wonder, their variety. They appeared as if they were whispering and laughing and lifting their heads with a shy pride. I felt many a time before that the trees had secrets between themselves. If we believe that they are unsocial beings, this only shows our stupidity and blindness and deafness. Oh that the Saviour would touch our eyes and enable us to see not men like trees walking but trees like men praying.

I enjoyed the meetings today. But I feel sometimes that there is a similarity between the pleasure which a Christian has in the 'Union' and the pleasure which the pagans of the old Roman Empire had when they went to see the combats in the arena. Fair play. The gladiators did their work extremely well today.

24 May (Tuesday)

Oh Lord God of Providence, who led the children of Israel out of the land of Egypt, and the Philistines from Caphtor, and the Syrians from Kir, lead our dear Wales in these days. You have kept her from century to century; you showed her the joy of your kingdom; you nurtured within her saints and apostles and reformers. You caused her to fail in power and to increase in grace. It is not Your Will that she is ending in shame without speaking to the nations. You gave her the message of peace and the Prince of Peace. Pour Your Spirit on her now. Speak through her to a world paralysed by fear. Fill her with Your love so that she may serve Your kingdom in freedom. Through Jesus Christ, King of the nations and King of the world.

*

A general election, as well as the Union, is claiming attention. Let the revolution come, the revolution of the Holy Spirit!

25 May (Wednesday)

It is good to hear a man speaking plainly from his heart. The lineage of the prophets is not finished. 'The truth against the world': there is no more attractive proverb in any language.

26 May (Thursday)

I said goodbye to friends and returned home in the company of a friend to vote, praying.

It is not inappropriate to meditate on sin when listening to the earliest results coming over the airwaves.

I noticed the list of the Seven Deadly Sins in the old book known as *Yn y llyvyr hwnn.*[13]

Arrogance or pride
Envy or jealousy
Hatred or anger
Apathy or laziness
Meanness or miserliness
Gluttony
Adultery or unchastity

The analysis under the seven headings is also interesting. But I will not pursue the sins of the 'flesh' which I have already considered. And as the news of the election pours into my room, I am compelled to think of the sins of the 'world'. The sin that belongs to the world is love of money according to some of the ancient authors, but the lust for worldly power is equally central. Here, of course, 'worldly' sin approximates to pride which is often considered the chief sin of the Devil. But we must differentiate between them. I know men who are not exceptionally proud but who have an insatiable lust for worldly power, the power to rule other people's lives. In these people, the naked will has swollen, as the whole personality has been constrained to serve one purpose, which is to subdue others to be servants of the tyrannous self. Perhaps 'lust' is the best word for worldly sin.

How guilty are you, the Brother of Low Degree?

27 May (Friday)

> *Oh Jesus Christ, help me to see and to hate my sin. Show me that I cannot serve God and Mammon. Lead me along the road that was sanctified by your work and sacrifice.*

I saw Jesus on the highway of history. He raised his hand and invited me towards the horizon.

CHAPTER 8

AVARICE

28 May (Saturday)

Iolo Goch[1] has his own list of the Seven Sins – 'the deadly seven deathly sins':

> *Pride* is our habit,
> *Anger, miserliness, laziness,*
> *Jealousy* often present,
> *Adultery,* woe to him who knows it;
> *Gluttony* of the voracious lips
> Not pleasant, but not me, I know.

If there is no comfort in the list, there is comfort in the praise for sacrifice that one finds in the same poem:

> Despite his memory, despite his mind,
> Despite his pain over the five ages of the world,
> Despite his portrayal of light,
> Which he made and brought to us,
> Despite having to face Friday,
> Despite his great pain and the spear,
> He bought heaven for us.

This is the only way to conquer sin: the Love that dwells in the universe which is higher and deeper and wider than everything in the universe, the Love of the Cross, the saving Sacrifice which will burn on the altar of Eternity – before a star was lit and after the sun is extinguished now and for ever.

29 May (Whitsun)

Oh Spirit who has been moving over the waters, come to me. Rush on me, the prison-free Wind, from north and south, from east and west. Snatch me from the midst of impurity and the sickness of the unclean crowds, elevate me to the mountain top of your holiness, blow on me, cleanse me, give me strength and a new life. You are the Fresh Air of heaven. Bless me with your vigour and liveliness and daring. You who blow through the desert of the Temptation and through the upper room of the Saints, shock Your Church with Your Presence, and make me live before You.

The difference between the disciples who fled from the garden of Gethsemane and the disciples who faced the crowd on the day of Pentecost is surprising.

30 May (Monday)

A friend recently told me that Dr Davies, Tre-lech,[2] used to say that love of money is the only sin that time does not tame. Perhaps that exceptional man was speaking from experience. It is often claimed that old age weakens the passions of the flesh and that experience teaches some degree of wisdom even to the most foolhardy, but much could be said to oppose both views. However, Davies, Tre-lech, claimed that love of money increased instead of decreasing.

Of course, there is more than one way of loving money. There is the traditional picture of the miser – the tightfisted, stingy person who watches over his goods with care, avoiding expenditure and giving nothing, accumulating wealth and hiding it nervously. This is Siôn Cent's picture:

He would rather...
The water rather than the wine from the inn,
The miser does not exact from his wealth
Only usury or profit taking.[3]

He is 'a dwarf of a man', similar to a mole. But there are other kinds of money lovers – like the one who seeks money since he has put his mind on the things which money can buy, luxuries and worldly comforts and a high life, and the one who handles money to enjoy the worldly power which money can give him, the power to lord it over the fate of men and nations. Of these two kinds of loving money the first comes close to being a sin of the flesh, the craving for splendid luxury, and there is a hint of this in the characters of Barabas in Marlowe's *Jew of Malta* and in Sir Epicure Mammon in Ben Jonson's *The Alchemist*. This boastful craving troubled many at the time of the Renaissance. The second kind of love of money is a particular form of the lust for worldly power. The influence of great financiers on the international troubles of our world has not so far been measured.

It is probable that Dr Davies, Tre-lech, was talking of this withered miserliness. The root of this is fear, the desire for safety. In the other kinds of love of money the desire for luxury and the desire for power can be seen.

*

My mind turns towards my Friend, one who never sought safety or luxury or power.

The gentle Jesus, let me come with you in my meditation along the roads of Palestine. Let me hear you announcing the blessing of the Kingdom to the poor and talking of the Treasure which neither moth nor rust can destroy nor thieves steal. Let me see the sunlight in your hair and the brooks in your voice. Let me see you as you are, Owner of all the wealth of the earth...

I came near to Jesus in my imagination. I saw the smile on his lips and the keenness of youth on his cheek, and I felt the brave and glorious love in his look as he embraced my soul. I was amazed at his amplitude and his poverty.

This is Evangelical Poverty, the Poverty of God, the Poverty which is opulent beyond the greedy musings of all the worshippers of Mammon.

31 May (Tuesday)

Some time ago I read a sentimental booklet about the three children in Portugal whose experiences provided a basis for the Roman Catholic cult concerning 'Our Lady of Fatima'. It was evident that there was some mass superstition associated with the cult and that its devotion had been perverted to feed enmity against Russian Communism. I'm afraid that I failed to see much glory in the children. But a priestly friend of mine was kind enough to give me a copy of a better book on the event, a book by C C Martindale.[4] What stayed with me after I had read it was the character of the boy Francisco and his growth in grace and his desire to 'comfort' God in the face of man's sin. Blessed be the little soul and his daring theology. 'If my soul desires God...'[5] The Love of God demolishes grammar and dogmatics.

1 June (Wednesday)

I have been searching my soul again to find out how guilty I am of money-loving sins. But I have failed to find the little devil of the love of money so far. I try to defend myself instead of acknowledging my fault. And it is not difficult for a minister to defend himself in this matter. Nearly every minister could get a much 'better living' in other work. Lust for money does not attract anyone to the ministry. The minister's work is a strange work: work that demands public and intellectual talents, work which, usually, demands long training in colleges, and work which gains for the worker an honourable proletariat wage. God save us all from complaining. But the truth stands: no one today enters the ministry to gain a completely comfortable economic position, free of care.

But I know that I am justifying myself.

2 June (Thursday)

The glory of the ministry remains, despite the unworthiness of the saints, and of the ministers themselves. How glad I am today of being able to greet a young minister with the prophetic fire burning in him.

3 June (Friday)

'You cannot serve God and mammon.' 'Therefore, I say to you, do not worry about the food and drink that you need; or about clothes for your body. After all, isn't life worth more than food? And isn't the body worth more than clothes?'⁶

CHAPTER 9

Mammon

4 June (Saturday)

Even when attempting to discuss mammon my soul wriggles, and the same old discomfort, the old feeling of guilt, gnaws at my heart. The Great Accuser looks at me all the while. I say 'even' because I am sometimes tempted to think that this is the least of sins in my life. The self-justification that is within me can be quite eloquent on the subject. And yet I feel guilty when I think of the Eternal Goodness who created me for goodness.

Let self-justification speak up for a little while. I am a minister of the Gospel. What lover of money would choose that calling? Could not every minister in our day earn a more comfortable living by doing other work? I recall a friend once calling me a fool and telling me of carefree jobs and incomes with much less work. I was once told that the obvious duty of every man is to earn sufficient wages to guarantee a good nurture and a deserving education for his children and that I was failing in my duty. 'If a man wishes to live in holy poverty, he should not beget children,' so said that accuser. I cannot see any strength in the argument at all, since good nurture and a deserving education depend on many more important things than money. But supposing that there is some strength in the argument, it is not the sin of loving money that is condemned by it.

I tried to divide love of money into three parts: desiring money for the sake of security, desiring money for the sake of luxury, desiring money for the sake of gaining power over other people. My particular guilt does not lie with the last two forms of love of money. If I tried to control the lives of others it was not through money that I did this. And I have not desired many luxuries either. Usually I am satisfied with the simple necessities, and even when I ventured from time to time to spend money on some unnecessary thing, my weakness was in the spending not in greed for money. Here the self-justifier is on more solid ground. But to what degree am I guilty of seeking security from need and loss at the expense of more important things? Am I less generous and less adventurous than I ought to be because of economic worry? Am I completely honest? Is the struggle to live taking too much of my energy and weighing too much on my mind?

5 June (The Lord's Day)

It is said that hospitality among Christians is becoming scarcer, and acquiring hospitality for ministers is burdensome for officers in some churches. It is easy to see that many families are very reluctant to welcome preachers. A good number are afraid of 'the revered, fearful calling'.

But amongst those who open their doors to their homes to wandering ministers the unending generosity is astonishing. Gratitude is my response every time. So it is today. The welcome was warm and thorough despite the ill-health of the kind lady of the house – an illness that could have provided sufficient excuse for refusing accommodation if it were not for the generosity of will there.

Strangely the conversation turned to financial contributions to the church. Here, also, this particular family is exceptionally generous. But it was not difficult to mention others who contributed much more to the cinema than the church.

Gospel, salvation, reconciliation, faith, brotherliness, communion of saints... Collection, treasury, pensions, subscriptions, sum total, audited and accepted as correct... 'So then, my dear brothers and sisters, stand firm and steady. Keep busy always in your work for the Lord... Now concerning the collection for God's people... You must do what I told the churches of Galatia to do.'[1]

Today is Trinity Sunday. I spoke of Incarnation, Atonement, Resurrection, the Holy Spirit.

Salvation must be paid for, and yet it must be received cheaply. There is value in the ancient doctrinal categories, and yet they testify to their own insufficiency!

6 June (Monday)

> Justice says 'Enough'!
> And the Father shouts 'Sufficient'!
> In the Atonement.[2]

Justice and its scales, the Father and his unfailing accounts, Surety and Balance Sheets... It is only God who is honest enough to take care of the Redemption!

7 June (Tuesday)

What a masterpiece of irony is 'Psalm to Mammon' by John Morris Jones.[3]

> You are stronger than Christ in the land of the Christian,
> Than the Buddha in India far across the seas;
> Than the desert land of Arabia that gives its heart,
> Not to Muhammad, but to Mammon.
>
> What do gifts and talents matter
> Compared with interest and rent books?
> Who is the man who has the gifts?
> He is servant to the one with a golden purse.
> (The BBC for example)
>
> 'Your neighbour,' says Nobody,
> 'You should love as yourself',
> He was a dreamer and poet,
> And he had a wild imagination,
> In brief, 'impractical' –
> Not easy to follow.

But as for the gospel of Mammon,
How totally different this!
How great, how 'practical';
Not difficult to follow.

O God, keep my hands clean, keep my heart pure. Through the
Pauper who died on the Cross. Amen.

The poet confesses that he has sinned against Mammon.

I gave a hundredfold
To the needy,
Or to the unworthy, without thought;
To pleaders who begged
I shared with those,
Instead of punishing them in the bailiff's cell.

Always prodigal,
Foolishly wasteful,
Neglectful, mistaken, I experienced loss;
I did not pressurize the weak,
The lowly I did not abuse,
Prizes I did not demand, I lost every bounty.

I am also tempted to boast in this vein. Giving thoughtlessly, spending without heeding, failing to sell anything, despising the winners of prizes and big wages – that has been my history. But before I start to boast I must face two accusations. One is that I have been careless about money because the old Adam within me is interested in other things. I expect that I will have to admit that this accusation is correct when I examine my sin further. The other accusation is that poverty, after I married and had children, has sent me to bend the knee occasionally in the temple of Mammon. I must consider that accusation.

8 June (Wednesday)

The Self-accuser and the Self-defender have been conversing without words, but to this end: You received an appeal for financial support for needy children in Europe. What about it? –My wife sends clothes to lighten the burden of one family on the continent. –Are you happy with your contribution to the Sustenance Fund?[4] –I would love to give more, but rearing children is proving more expensive every day. –What have you done concerning the other appeals that came to you recently: Missionary Work, The Ecumenical Movement, Parliament for Wales, peace movements, election fund, eisteddfod, widows' fund, a memorial fund, the college here and the library there...? –Ministers receive more appeals than anyone else but receive a lower wage than most. One must judge between different needs. –Why did you not give more? –I cannot afford more. We have a struggle to live on my income without being able to save a halfpenny towards the education of the children or any crisis that might arise. –Perhaps you are spending too much on food and clothes. –Taranwen believes in good food. We do not have unnecessary delicacies. The children have never tasted Christmas turkey. If the children's clothes are in good trim, thanks are due for the kindness of Taranwen's mother and warm-hearted friends. Taranwen does not spend enough on clothes for herself. I have only the necessities, with neither a spare tie nor a sock. –You are beginning to get enthusiastic, my friend. But is it not better to wear sackcloth than spend money on clothes when brothers and sisters endure famine and nakedness in far-off lands? –I have no answer to this question.

9 June (Thursday)

We had a busy and pleasant day. If I am seeing Mammon everywhere at the moment, the fault is mine. It was an encouragement to hear a speech declaring with eloquence the romantic values of the Old Welsh as a basis for preaching today.

10 June (Friday)

I have to attend more and more committees these days. Come to think of it, Mammon is an industrious member of every committee.

11 June (Saturday)

I enjoy historical films – even the most unhistorical ones. When a close friend told me that *Quo Vadis* was worth seeing, I took the opportunity; and indeed, even despite the fact that the makers of the film were determined to satisfy our desire to give a hefty blow to the ones we are cross with, the challenge of the Christian faith came through: the disciples of the unyielding Love standing gloriously up to the persecuting powers. If this is Christianity, then the majority of the world's Christians are not Christians at all. Am I being too harsh?

12 June (The Lord's Day)

I had to sit with the kind folk at my accommodation last night to watch television.

'Aren't the standards of the programmes extremely low?' one of them said, still gazing on the moving picture.

'Yes,' concurred another, 'I can't understand the state of mind of the people who are responsible for them.'

'Of course, you can turn off the tasteless programme, if you want,' said the first.

'Yes, of course you can,' said the second. 'But if you have no standards, you cannot judge between the good and bad. This kind of stuff does not do any harm to people like us, but I am shocked when I think of the effect that programmes like this have on people that lack any standards.'

'Yes, that's the trouble,' said the other.

The three of us remained watching the screen until the programme ended.

Today I felt, as I led the services, that centuries of Christian fellowship were behind me. The particular church had been celebrating its one-hundred-and-fiftieth anniversary, but the history of every church is part of the history of the one Great Church, the Church gathered from every nation, every tribe and language. The inchoate prayers of the saints filled the meeting house.

Gracious Lord, anchor our faith, fulfil our dreams, exceed our requests. Through the man who was once under nails. Amen.

Our public prayers are full of platitudes. There is one platitude I always enjoy, and that is 'Exceed our requests'. We would be impoverished if God did not do that.

13 June (Monday)

I haven't read any exposition which attempts to suggest what happened to Ananias and Sapphira after they had fallen dead following the judgement of the apostle and of their own conscience. If I were the Avenging Angel I would give them a particular punishment, to condemn them to wander the earth and keep them from entering heaven until they came across a Christian who would always fill in his tax return with total honesty.

That would be a somewhat difficult task, and a lengthy one.

A cold war always exists between every tax payer and the tax collecting authority. This is taken for granted. I have not heard of anyone, not even the Chancellor of the Exchequer, who expects a person to fill in his return at a disadvantage to himself. Everyone understands that every wise person 'claims' every allowance which is allowed. I am somewhat unwise. But it is possible to be unwise without being – what word can I use – innocent.

It is one thing to claim an allowance; it is another to declare income in detail on a form. How many Christians declare the truth, the whole truth and nothing but the truth? Those daring Christians who elevate 'Absolute Truth' and 'Absolute Honesty' as standards for their lives, how much eagerness do they have for filling their tax form?

Of course, one must be flexible. If a kindly neighbour gives half a crown to be spent by the children on a Sunday school trip, the father is not expected to note the fact on the form, as far as I know. If the Angelic Recorder in the Court of Heaven is keeping careful accounts of the occasional gifts and earnings which cheer the hearts of all the ministers in Wales, he must have a more numerous staff than the income tax authorities have in Wales. That richly resourced programmer whose name is so frequently in the *Radio Times*, that champion at the special preaching rallies whose name is advertised so prominently in tall letters on churches' posters, that industrious minister who has learned thoroughly the art of buying in the cheapest market, and selling in the dearest: will they be blushing, I wonder, on the Day of Judgement, when they see all the income tax forms they had filled set in a mischievous row in front of them?

What will you say on the Day of Judgement, you Brother of Low Degree? That you are less flexible than many? That you work harder and for a lesser wage than most of your contemporaries? That society is indebted to you? That even the prophet must have a living? Probably. I am beginning to know you.

14 June (Tuesday)

I tried to imagine the glory of God's Victory: the shining white Throne, the Sea of Glass, the glittering angels, the blessed saints in their white clothes, the Lamb who was slain. And to be fair to my fatigued memory – the scene was beyond the powers of Cecil B de Mille and the Archbishop of Canterbury to produce anything similar. But when I attempted to look at myself, I saw that I was one of the grey and fearful souls standing at the rear of a number of uneasy souls who were waiting their turn to appear before the winged and august Recorder. As I approached him at the back of the crowd I could overhear his remarks about every one.

'This is a Christian who had a profound experience in a service but was very careful, when it came to the collection, to choose a sixpenny piece rather than half-a-crown.'

'This is a Christian who refused to spend more than three shillings on a Christmas present for the child of an old friend because the old friend had not spent more than three shillings on a gift for his child the previous Christmas.'

'This is a Christian who used to study the financial report of his church very carefully every year in order to avoid giving more to the cause than other members who had similar wages to him.'

The vision faded before I took my place before the all-knowing Recorder. And there was total darkness.

15 June (Wednesday)

Oh Lord, save me, from the bottomless pit, from the slime and rot,
from self-righteousness and self-deceit, from Beelzebul and Mammon,
from scratching and grasping, save me, oh save me.
Cleanse me and I will be clean.

16 June (Thursday)

I tried to think of Jesus' refusal to adjudge in the case of the man who had a complaint against the injustice of his brother. I tried to think of him looking at the penny and saying, 'Pay the Emperor what belongs to the Emperor, and pay God what belongs to God.'[5] I tried to think of him wandering the country, homeless, doing good and telling his disciples to go out in defenceless poverty to preach the Gospel of God's Kingdom. His will for me became clearer.

17 June (Friday)

'Do not store riches for yourselves here on earth... but store up riches for yourselves in heaven... For your heart will always be where your riches are.'[6]

18 June (Saturday)

I am wrestling with Mammon in a particular way these days. Rather thoughtlessly, I accepted an invitation to important and attractive conferences. Since the authorities who invited me were offering to pay my travelling expenses it was too good an opportunity to miss in order to do theology and to meet fellow theologians in continental countries. But there are other expenses apart from travel expenses, and I can now see clearly that it is impossible to go without having financial support from somewhere. In the crisis I remember monies that I had earned some time back but have not been paid to me by the two institutions I served. Two institutions, not two persons – but it is extremely distasteful having to write two letters to ask, hesitatingly and kindly, whether some of my earnings could be paid, and offering extra services in the future as a way of thanking them for help in times of trouble.

There is nothing more demeaning than asking for money, even money which on some counts is owing to me. But the really painful thing is to ask for money from someone who is in need, even if you feel that your need at the moment is more acute.

Have I asked for my shirt back instead of giving my coat as well? My only consolation is that there is no mention of going to law on one side or the other.

The Christian life is the opposite of washing in dirt.

19 June (The Lord's Day)

'The hungry he filled with good things and sent the rich away with empty hands.'

'He has sent me to bring good news to the poor, to heal the

broken hearted, to proclaim liberty to the captives and recovery of sight to the blind, to set free the oppressed, and to announce that the time has come when the Lord will save his people.'

Luke's Gospel is a miracle of a book. We should pay more attention to the Sermon on the Plain.

'Happy are you poor; the Kingdom of God is yours.'

'Happy are you who are hungry now; you will be filled.'

'Happy are you who weep now, you will laugh.'

'Give to others and God will give to you. Indeed you will receive a full measure, a generous helping, poured into your hands – all that you can hold. The measure that you use for others is the one that God will use for you.'[7]

20 June (Monday)

Our circumstances are so constrained that I have gone to some trouble from time to time to gain exceedingly small amounts. But it is clear that I have no talent to snatch at opportunities to make large amounts of money. Something always prevents me. I get more satisfaction from writing a few lines for Welsh-language newspapers with little or no fees than in writing anything in English. I often feel that I ought to lighten the economic burden on the family by writing something in English, and the English literary figures in Wales are not fully aware of their opportunities; but my experience to date is that it is difficult for me to write anything in English without feeling disloyal to Wales and the Welsh language.

21 June (Tuesday)

We have been discussing our financial difficulties today. I recognize that I cannot attend the conferences on the Continent without curtailing some of the family's necessities. I regret now my thoughtless decision to grasp the opportunity to visit foreign countries in the company of theologians and denominational leaders.

After I had discussed the matter a wave of carping dissatisfaction came over me. 'I do not ask for a life of luxury' – but in the name of all fairness ought not our burden be a little less? Should it not be possible for me to get books and an occasional journey to historical centres in Europe without stealing clothes off the children's backs? I began to think of other families who have plenty of money to spend on trash, and we have to skimp and scrape. And we are so deserving! I don't suppose it's difficult for anyone to think that he is more deserving than the occasional fellow pilgrim.

But the Accuser came to look me in the eye. His form was shapeless but the terror of his grandeur overcame my soul. Suddenly, Christ was looking at me, gently and with mercy and his unending strength flowed over my life.

*

I have no words to describe my feeling of shame – nor the joy, either, knowing that Jesus of Nazareth was my friend and companion.

'Foxes have holes, and birds have nests, but the Son of Man has nowhere to lie down and rest.'[8]

22 June (Wednesday)

Old books on ethics draw a distinction between debts which one hopes to pay and debts which there is no hope of paying. An old minister told me once that he and his wife had decided at the start of their married life that they would never buy anything without paying for it so that a bill would never arrive at their home. I admire the decision of the conscientious couple, but I have never felt that it is a sin to take out a loan, or to receive goods without paying immediately when the occasion arises. But certainly one should never borrow without hope of paying and paying honourably in agreement with contract. Every debt is a burden, and the fact that the life of society by now is imbued with borrowing and interest and credit does not lighten it.

23 June (Thursday)

I see a road that opens now
Out of the world's massive corruption...
The road is Christ and his gift
And the Atonement that occurred on Calvary.[9]

The salvation in Christ is not one dramatic event, but a beneficent process of cleansing oneself and being sustained in his love: seeing the road and walking through mud and dust, over stones and pits and ditches.

Oh my Lord Jesus Christ, how completely incapable am I without the Eternal Love which was revealed on your cross. Lost in the vastness of the universe, lost in my own sin, lost in the corrupt complications of human life – that is my condition without you. Wash me in the waters of your sacrifice, purify my breath by the breeze of your peace.

24 June (Friday)

I am not as poor as I deserve.

'There is no one who has left home or brothers or sisters or father or mother or wife or children or lands, for my sake and the gospel, who will not receive much more in this present age – houses and brothers and sisters and mothers and children and lands, as well as persecutions; and eternal life in the age to come.'[10]

Thank God it is true.

25 June (Saturday)

Today it was a great pleasure to take McTavish and Flanagan to the seaside on the Sunday school trip, and Mrs Morgans, one of my neighbours, also entrusted her son Morys, into my care. Morys is skilful at shooting with a gun, and it was impossible to entice him away from the shooting stall until he had spent ten shillings and had won a small glass, which was broken on the way to the bus to return home. But the boy is kinder and more patient than our children, and we enjoyed his company very much. To be fair, our children were extremely amenable and the whole day was an unadulterated pleasure. I succeeded in forgetting every worry and threw myself into children's activities. I do not always succeed in achieving this. The hours passed like minutes.

A certain joy and a certain strange thankfulness entered my heart on the homeward journey. Laughing and crying, becoming acquainted with the life which is one another's tongues and breasts and legs – this is preferable to being Lord of the Universe without having anybody to respect you or fear you or to laugh at you.

Our life is worse than nothingness without one another.

26 June (The Lord's Day)

After the service this evening Taranwen and I had supper with wealthy friends who live in an old mansion which was bought by them a few years ago. We admired the house and its acreage and its expensive furniture, and were greatly interested in the history of the sales where some of the treasures had been bought.

When we arrived home we went to look at the children sleeping. McTavish is short-tempered and Flanagan is provocatively defiant and Ap Siencyn is as stubborn as a mule, and the three of them are slow and unsteady in their development. But I would not accept the gold of Peru in exchange for any of them.

Forgive the little sentimentality. Our wedding anniversary only arrives once a year. It was a joyous occasion to be able to have supper together in the house of friends.

27 June (Monday)

There are many meanings to the word 'will'. It can mean 'intent' only. It can mean that self-discipline which enables a man to achieve his aim. It can mean a rampant ambition. It can mean an insatiable desire to subdue and rule other people. The words 'good will' signify a general love towards the earth's inhabitants – in most of its contexts anyway. To will is not a sin. To will oppressively is the sin, to seek lordship over Creator and fellow creature.

I saw a man training a young dog to achieve remarkable deeds in complete obedience to its master's voice. The drill was painful for me. One of the most hurtful things for me was to see the look on the master's face; the desire for complete mastery, for the total submission of the animal. 'My will be done.' I saw the same look on the face of a father who was punishing his child. He was an unmanageable and disobedient child, ready to scream under every chastisement. The father demanded silence and shook the boy. The screams increased, and the father struck the child's face, and kept on striking until the frightful noise reverberated throughout the house. The mother had to put a stop to the madness to prevent lasting damage to the boy. The father stood amazed, having failed to impose his will on his son.

'My will be done.' God save us from violating souls.

28 June (Tuesday)

Hearing today of the healing ministry made me uncomfortable. In my ministry I tried within the powers of the Faith to give strength and healing and guidance occasionally, but I never ventured to compete with the doctor. I felt many times that we had limited too much the work of the healing ministry by differentiating too rigidly between the work of a minister and the work of the doctor. But until today the issue did not come to trouble me like a thorn. I neglected the healing power of prayer, failed to lead our people to pray together for our fellow man in a purposeful way, remained satisfied with the formalism and barrenness of our churches – could there be a more heart-rending sign of the failure of the minister?

I know that there are dangers in the healing ministry: the danger of cheating and self-deception, healing for a time, leaving disappointment and black unbelief behind, nurturing some insufficient idea of the meaning of the Faith – and the danger which Jesus himself saw: devoting oneself to healing bodies at the cost of saving souls and the world – 'turning salvation into sanitation', as a friend told me. But I also know that it is better to enable the lame to walk than to preach into the void.

29 June (Wednesday)

Failure, disappointment, futility, bitterness – I cannot escape from these.

> *Lord Jesus, I feel that I am withdrawing from you these days. Save me from the ebb and flow of my spiritual communion with you. Bind my soul with cords of your love. Now and for ever.*

Manasseh and Magdalene: I wonder if I am worthy of their company?

30 June (Thursday)

Here the Brother of Low Degree has finished six months of this diary.

In one sense I have departed from Christ and the Father during this period. I am not as certain, by a long way, of the Presence. The visitations only occur occasionally now, although they could be more intense when they come, but I have faced up to much of my sin, and I know that I am gradually revealing the hidden places of my soul. I am moving fearfully forward towards the most painful confessions and the baring of my soul before God. One half of my soul would wish to end the diary now; the other half would wish to continue until a conclusion is reached which will give me satisfaction – or a warning to others.

I believe that some readers of the diary think that it has lasted too long already and that it is now a burden and a plague. The occasional person thinks of some numbskull who is making a show of feelings and transgressions which should be properly out of sight. I, personally, am perfectly certain that a pattern is forming in the narrative, and that, before long, I will have to face a decision which will be healing for me or will break me.

1 July (Friday)

I am a father. When one of my children puts his hand into my hand or rests his head on my shoulder, a thrill of happy longing and humble pride runs through me.

Father God, teach me to give my all to them and for them without violating their wills or lives. Through Jesus Christ my Brother. Amen.

2 July (Saturday)

On my way to keep an engagement I lingered in Neath market to look at the second-hand books. A man approached me smelling of drink. He readily conceded that he had drunk a little, and went on to say that he had something important to tell me. The important thing came out of his mouth five or six times before he departed, and the message was – and of course I had heard it many times before – 'what counts is not what you know but who you know'. Accepting that his English was inaccurate, his tone was earnest and his eyes glinted. He spoke as one who had returned from the realm of death.

The proverb which he announced so passionately has become too familiar recently, and the meaning is that knowing influential people is more important for a man who hopes for a job than all the knowledge he might possess, that pulling strings is more important than every merit. But the strange earnestness of the man gave me the impression that he was giving another meaning to the words. I made some friendly noises to encourage him to enlarge and explain; but instead of that he confessed that he had drunk too much and he repeated the words again with the soul's conviction in his voice.

Knowing is not the great blessing, but being acquainted with a person, and being acquainted with God; the old antithesis between the Tree of Knowledge and the Tree of Life.

3 July (The Lord's Day)

'Our Father, who art in heaven, hallowed be Thy name, Thy Kingdom Come. Thy will be done, on earth, as it is in heaven…'

Oh God, my Lord, the Speaker and the Word and the Breath of the Speaker, bless my will to serve Your will. I kneel confused before You as I remember the first 'Let it be' that my mind can feebly comprehend; as I remember the wonders of the universe; as I remember the miracles of growth and maturity and giving birth and perishing; as I remember man's strength and imagination and ability; as I remember the blessed commandment which ensures that evil is destructive and love is creative; as I remember the Cross; as I remember the lineage of the prophets and the men of wisdom and the missionaries and all the acts of the Holy Spirit; as I remember Your gentleness and patience; as I remember your unfettered industry; as I remember your non-violent will. Let Your will be done in me, in Your Church and in Your World. For Yours is the Kingdom. Amen.

CHAPTER 10

ON A JOURNEY

4 July (Monday)

Today I must start my journey to the Continent.[1] Raising a sufficient sum to undertake this journey has occasioned some grief, but somehow or other here I am ready to start, and Taranwen and Anna are full of advice and good wishes and full of gentleness and sweetness as well. They are better than I deserve.

I felt uncomfortable and even guilty on leaving the family for over a month. It means leaving all the work and responsibility for the family mainly to Taranwen, and the battle for the language also: forgetful and playful MacTavish; talkative, slow and stubborn Ap Siencyn whose fist is heavier than his intention; and Flanagan, a perfect daughter of Eve if ever there was one. Leaving all for a twelfth part of a year – it is no wonder that something is troubling my conscience.

Is it about time that I see a little of the Continent? No; it is not about time to do anything except repent. But will not the conference enable me to bear witness to some of the values of Christ and Wales? We shall see.

5 July (Tuesday)

I do not intend giving an account of the journey. It would be unfair to keep a diary not only for myself but also for my two fine fellow travellers. I feel that Welsh Congregationalism is safe in their hands if I fail. I fear every conference. Fortunately, the organizational knowledge of one companion and the theological brilliance of the other ascertain that the voice of Wales will be clearly heard.

But it was a pleasure to travel across the channel and through France with these two. On the whole, the inhabitants of the Continent are more careful than us Welsh to beautify and clean their countries. We ought not to be so complacent about our dusty stations and all the vulgar advertisements which defile our roads. The houses in France vary, at least in the parts of the country which I saw – I'm afraid that I slept in the train as I was conveyed through the industrial areas. What is wrong with us in Wales? I cannot accept the foolish idea that we are inherently lacking in the ability to see and create visual beauty. The true reason, I am certain, is that we lack the conviction that we are responsible for her. We have been used to leaving the responsibility of caring for our country to people who have no interest in Wales as the home of a particular nation.

It was a pleasure to note so much 'rank individualism' even among the telegraph poles in France – as in other countries on the Continent. The stupid uniformity of the telegraph poles in Wales and England are somehow constricting. In France the poles look like young, naked trees which have escaped from the forest to run a mischievous race along the road – the strong and the feeble, the thick and the thin, some leaning on each other and others prancing ahead by themselves.

6 July (Wednesday)

A number of more or less Congregational bodies are represented in this conference in Le-Chambon-sur-Lignon, and it is good that they have come together to exchange thoughts and experiences.

It is strange what a mixture of feeling comes over me on looking around at the interesting gathering that is here – Americans and Englishmen and Dutchmen and one German and a Swede and, of course, a good number of Frenchmen. It is a comic scene from one view; but my urge to laugh is complicated by feelings of dislike or of attraction to some. And yet, when I look from one to the other, a painful tenderness enters my heart and I say to myself, 'Here are the children of the King trying to live together.'

7 July (Thursday)

We must convince man of his sin – and of his dignity. In the past, much of the theology of the Church has degraded man instead of saving him. One cannot call a man a poor worm and at the same time convince him of sin. His sin is that he has rejected God and rejected the divine image in himself. One cannot really talk of sin without talking of the *Imago Dei*.

The doctrine of the Fall is one of the most comforting doctrines.

8 July (Friday)

There is an unmistakeable delight in a heated theological debate. The temptation is to try and win the argument or at least to make an effective contribution to it – and to lose sight of the Way and the Truth and the Life. It is easy to find fault with others. May the Holy Spirit guide me to the Truth which is greater than me.

9 July (Saturday)

As I travelled third class on the French railways from Le-Chambon-sur-Lignon to St Etienne I could not but think that I was one of the poor. The carriage was so uncomfortable and unattractive. On arriving at Geneva and noticing the prices of the clothes and other goods in the shops in the street which led from the main railway station to the famous lake I became convinced that I am one of the poor in fact and in truth. But I adored the city. Strange the providence which has made it the capital city of diplomacy.

10 July (The Lord's Day)

Some of us were able to see John Calvin's chair this morning, and his pulpit (although only its sounding board is really old) in the austere main church of St Pierre. Moving from the street of expensive luxuries to this austere house of worship meant changing religion and changing epochs.

The will, the black, pitiless, unforgiving will, the will which will tame and sentence the flesh and creation – is not this the essence of Calvin's religion? The will of the Great King in law and purpose, the will of the quaking subject rejecting and being petrified under the authority of the Eternal Church, the will of the withered reformer tightening his grip on the city in the face of threats by armed kingdoms and enemies within and without – is that the whole story? No, the flame and the kiss and the faithfulness must also be remembered.

11 July (Monday)

And now a week of committee meetings is ahead of us, in one of the centres of the Ecumenical Movement.[2] Some say that this is one of the purest manifestations of the guidance of the Holy Spirit in our age. But it can't be denied that it is also a choice way of combining duty and pleasure. The only price that needs to be paid is a little formal piety. I do not wish to speak disrespectfully of any act of joint worship; but if I am to be totally honest, I must confess that my mind tends to wander when I hear someone leading intercessions and expecting me to pray for a series of occupations like this: 'Let us pray, firstly, for those who are owners of offices and factories... (a few minutes of silent prayer)... secondly, for those who hold important positions in offices and shops... thirdly, for those who hold lower posts in offices and factories... fourthly, for those who are drawing to the end of their service in offices and factories...' and so on. There is a difference between breath and Breath in glory. Thank God, the feeling and passion of the true prayer is in the conference chaplain's evening service.

'A toi la gloire, o Ressuscité...'[3]

12 July (Tuesday)

At a conference like this, one is able to begin a meaningful relationship with fellow conferees quite quickly, even those who had been total strangers to him previously. Within a day he considers so-and-so as a friend or ally and someone else as an enemy to be defeated or to be wary of. Sometimes, the relationship is much more complicated. There is one who through long acquaintance and warm-hearted enough occasions is considered as some kind of friend but who is fighting fiercely on the other side of the debate; and there's another one who is also an opponent but who presents his case so effectively and so courteously that he wins admiration and affection.

That is a great deal of complication even in a short time, and within a fairly small company. It is good to see that the three Welshmen who are here are a great support to each other.

13 July (Wednesday)

From time to time in this diary I have attempted to acknowledge some of my sin. There is a considerable amount that has not been acknowledged yet. But it is not my intention to talk of the sins of the past. The sin that is – that's the topic – the sinful condition of my soul now. I am not attempting to write a confessional autobiography, but a diary of my soul in its present experience.

And yet I will also have to beware of making the diary an escape from the past. At this conference I feel how easy it is to be lost, to some degree, in a make-believe world. Novelists and dramatists often speak of the weight of past guilt weighing on some creature like some vengeful fate, and the wretch failing to forget, failing to find release. The testimony of my experience is very different. There is nothing easier for me than to forget unpleasantness.

As a child and youth I spent a lot of time daydreaming, imagining that I accomplished feats or gained some kind of ascendancy. I now realize that dreaming in this way is a waste of energy that I cannot afford. It is rarely that I now sink into such dreams. But there is in me a similar tendency which is as strong as ever – the tendency to throw the unpleasant into oblivion and to enjoy and relive pleasant experiences. The after-taste of 'good times' in the pulpit or on a platform can last longer than the after-taste of an onion or herring. When I remember some foolishness or failure it causes me genuine pain – pain which is sometimes expressed in groaning which can be heard – but on the whole I succeed wonderfully in keeping unpleasant memories out of my consciousness.

Moving in the small world of the conference causes me to realize how easy for me it is to 'live in the present' and to ignore the unity which is between me and that scoundrel who betrayed his God as often as his own friend. I must face my own history.

14 July (Thursday)

Oh Eternal Lord, who has known me as child, as youth, as man, do not let me forget that changeable Self who sinned against you. Remind me of the lives that I have harmed and the glories which I have desecrated. Teach me to repent, not to ignore. Do not hide anything from my sight. Show me every tear and every blush, every ruination and every loss. Renew my soul in Christ Jesus. Amen.

15 July (Friday)

This conference came to an end. I had to say goodbye to my two fellow Welshmen. We had an agreeable time. If we saw theologians baring their teeth, we also experienced the true fellowship.

16 July (Saturday)

Following the departure of my colleagues I was very lonely. I recall the time when I used to despise people who could not be alone – modern man to whom loneliness was a bugbear.

At that time I was proud of my own shyness; I remember a friend calling me 'A Lone Wolf'. I had respect for the prophet who could face the loneliness of the desert in the company of his God, and I had greater respect at that time for the self-possessed and self-sufficient man who could challenge God and abject humans and bring shame and pain, like Prometheus in the fable, in his own heroic strength. I learnt a lot through experience; and, although I still have the deepest respect for the prophet and the hero who can face loneliness, I know that the achievement is impossible without the strength of the Almighty. Part of the meaning of the cry from the Cross, 'My God, why did you abandon me?'[4] is the experience of extreme loneliness and this is not a thing to be talked about lightly. Here I am experiencing a fairly unpleasant time, and there are plenty of people always around me. I long for the home which I left less than a fortnight ago and to which I will return in less than three weeks time.

17 July (The Lord's Day)

I was present this morning at the service for a child's baptism. It was done neatly, but as a symbolic act sprinkling is wholly inadequate compared with immersion. There is a lot to be said for not using water at all; there is something to be said for using sufficient to cover the whole body: but there is nothing to be said for using a little water for the sake of convenience.

The usual thoughts entered my heart: thought for the child and its parents, for the opportunities of life, for the condition of the world; I prayed for this little one and every one of God's children; I confessed my own sin.

The years that have passed rose like unrelenting witnesses against me. Waste, destruction, loss, chaos: they stand like a row of skeletons.

A verse comes to mind, one of the verses which has proved most charming to me all my life: 'I will give you back what you lost in the years when swarms of locusts ate your crops. It was I who sent this army against you.' The theology of the verse is enough to make every philosopher of religion giddy. It is a pleasure to turn to the strange portion of Joel's prophecy and read on to the renowned words: 'Afterwards I will pour out my spirit on everyone: your sons and daughters will proclaim my message; your old people will have dreams, your young people will see visions...'[5]

18 July (Monday)

I am now on a journey once more. I had a glimpse of the modernity of Lausanne and an exceptionally pleasant glimpse of the remarkable beauty of Bern. Bern is sufficient proof that shops can be an adornment of a culture, and that a capital city can be a heritage. Of course, it is a toy city. Perhaps Switzerland is a toy country. I never saw anything more toy-like than the soldiers, anyway. Since I am leaving Geneva to make enough room for the Big Four,[6] one can but hope that they do something to make toys of all the soldiers in the world.

I arrived, at last, in Zürich and received a warm welcome from friends. It is not often that a theologian-poet is welcomed to a home where the wife is a poet and the husband a theologian. I had met their daughter previously, but this was the first time for me to meet the parents. It was the poetess's night tonight. She took me out to see the lights of Zürich at night. Tomorrow, apparently, I will have the company of the theologian to see some of the historical buildings associated with Zwingli and Bullinger.[7] As I drank a cup of coffee beneath the branches of a tree by a soothing fountain I learnt that Zürich was one of the most morally 'puritanical' cities in Switzerland.

19 July (Tuesday)

The poet and the theologian were my companions on my short pilgrimage to some of the sacred places associated with Zwingli and Bullinger – and Gottfried Keller.[8] After I had resisted the temptation to carve my name on the woodwork in Keller's tavern and after I had bowed my head on seeing Rahab, Ruth, Bathsheba and Mary together on one of the doors of the Grossmunster, I had to depart from Zurich in sadness. But I enjoyed the journey from there to München: hearing the cattle bells near some stations, being amazed at the whiteness of the snow-clad peaks in the distance, noticing some strange difference between country and country when crossing a corner of Austria on the shore of the Bodensee, and my eagerness becoming heavier on approaching the ancient city of München and the dear ones who live there. And on arriving I received a warm welcome from Dorothea and Ricarda.

20 July (Wednesday)

In her present condition the city is a strange memorial to the pomp of princes and to the wickedness of war: to the glory of Europe and to the violence of *La Barbarie*. Neither one nor the other can be identified with any country. The creator and destroyer wrestle together in all our lives. It is comforting to think of the promises in the Testament which is on the table in my cell in the Roman Catholic *Hospiz* where I am staying.

> *Oh Lord, teach us to live. Make us worthy of the privilege of breathing. For it is from You that we received the breath of life into our nostrils. To You be the glory now and for ever.*

21 July (Thursday)

Palaces, monuments, artistic fountains, museums, a baroque church, gardens – I must spend a year in this place. I was driven by one benefactor to an exhibition of modern art and by another to the Tierpark, the animal park where the creatures usually enjoy a degree of natural freedom.

The exhibition was disappointing. I enjoyed about three of the artists, and when I explained their work to the young student who had advised me to visit the exhibition he told me that I was partial to some 'divinatory realism'. To tell the truth there is much more 'divinatory realism' in the other part of the Haus der Kunst which contains pictures by Dürer and Rembrandt and Rubens.

Wondering at the creatures in the Tierpark was a means of grace: ponies caressing each other; small goats receiving food from a child dwarf; cows from India looking so much like their grandmothers from Wales; monkeys indulging in their nether parts; the walrus and the penguin, close neighbours, parodying humanity; the zebra and the lion conveying two messages about beauty; the electric eel exemplifying adjustment with the environment. But it was strange to see lions and tigers behind bars, and the elephants, having played the mouth-organ, receiving gifts of money and transferring them immediately to the keeper. Mammon has all the gifts, as John Morris Jones said.

22 July (Friday)

I saw more churches and more paintings (Böcklin, Spitzweg and others in the Schack Galerie), and discussed Heart Break with Ricardo, looking in astonishment at the majestic beauty of Nymphenburg.

23 July (Saturday)

I am saddened as I think that this incomparable respite in München is coming to an end – and even now I cannot return home. I visited some of the churches for the second time – Bügersaal, Michaelskirche, Frauenkirche – and grieved about the destruction which had been and observed the signs of rebuilding. It comes to mind what Rehoboam did after Shishak, king of Egypt, had taken the gold shields of Solomon. 'To replace them, King Rehoboam made bronze shields.'[9] In one sense it is not possible to pay back the years destroyed by the locusts. However, nobody can but God. 'What I have written, stays written'[10]: proud and frightening words!

I also watched, a little after eleven o'clock in the morning, the human images weaving and dancing on the clock tower of the Neues Rathaus: a reflection of life for the hundreds of tourists who had been watching with me.

I enjoyed looking at some of the shops in the afternoon: ancient furniture, traditional clothes, and windows full of Chianti bottles. There is an art of living if only it could be mastered.

24 July (The Lord's Day)

I had plenty of time to think about people and things as I made the return journey to Geneva. I went out of my way between Zürich and Bern in order to catch a glimpse of Zug and Luzern. The loveliest scenes were the Swiss cottages between Luzern and Bern, although I was far from despising the lakes. It is certain that Luzern has great beauty, but it cannot be appreciated amidst swarms of pleasure seekers.

T H Parry-Williams mentions Lake Luzern in a poem which discusses religion, if I remember correctly. As I stood among the crowd and looked at the lake a sense of weariness came over me: a feeling unlike the tearful longing that came over the same poet according to the testimony of a poem in which he declares doubt ('I wept because the Godhead needed my tears'); a lot nearer my condition would be 'I spat because the Godhead needed my spittle.'[11] Am I unloving? At one time I had a strong tendency towards misanthropy. It is obvious that it has not withered completely yet. I am beginning to doubt whether I am sinking back into the fierce desert which was the spasmodic condition of my soul (the word be cursed) before I gained the continuous feeling of God's presence which I describe at the beginning of this diary.

The truth is that I cannot delete from my mind the memory of a painting which I saw in München, a painting of Jesus being abused by the soldiers, a work from the late Middle Ages. It was a painting of the insanity of cruelty and the stupidity of suffering, and nothing else, as far as I could see. And yet there is some truth to the declaration, and there have been times during the last twenty years when I have seen nothing but this. But I long for the full revelation.

Oh Wholeness, snatch me, lest the Non-existence catches me.

25 July (Monday)

I have a busy week ahead: delivering lectures every morning on sections of the Book of Acts which present the essential message of the earliest Christian preachers. I must lead discussion, answer questions and assist in the work of planning a course for about eighty theological students from many denominations and countries. Oh for grace to convey the majesty of the subject!

26 July (Tuesday)

When I was preparing the Greek texts to explain the Person of Christ I had to think of the disciples' experience of the Resurrected One, for that was the essence of salvation for the early Christians. Oh how wonderful if the Christ were to visit this fellowship of young theological students! But I do not feel the presence tonight in my own cell – not very closely, indeed. I am attempting to perceive Christ behind the rows of Greek letters.

27 July (Wednesday)

I will have to write my autobiography one day for my own sake if not for the sake of others. I am tempted to venture on an adjectival summary, like this –

The first year: greedy.
The second: greedy and fearful.
The third: greedy and fearful and moanful
The fourth: greedy and fearful and moanful and jealous.
The fifth: ... and stubborn.
The sixth: ... and dreamy.
The seventh: ... and sullen.
The eighth: ... the same but less sullen and more fastidious.

The ninth: ... and self-pitying.

The tenth: ... and cunning – increasingly so until my cunning comes to light.

The eleventh: ... moral awakening and becoming pharisaical.

The twelfth: ... full of fear at having to face the confusing and frightening world of the County School.

The thirteenth: ... the fear becoming nightmarish with the sexual agonies of youth.

The fourteenth: ... a strange religious experience lifted me into the seventh heaven, but following this, the awakening of my critical powers threw me into a pit of doubt.

The fifteenth: ... terror, blasphemy, self-hatred.

The sixteenth: ... beginning to think about poetry and settling into atheism.

The seventeenth: ... agnostic.

I notice that the chronicle has ceased to be adjectival; and making a list like this does not compel me to face my past. I have been feeding my egoism today. If this will be the essence of my autobiography, I had better not write it.

28 July (Thursday)

I had to face the multilingual Hydra of this conference and answer a host of questions this morning. One topic was raised in different forms time after time. Is there a beginning of evil in time? Is God a Saviour prior to sin appearing? Is there a contradiction in the nature of the Godhead? I did not succeed in convincing everyone by talking of Mystery.

29 July (Friday)

I received spiritual sustenance when I worshipped in the Orthodox Evensong which was held more than once during the conference. But I do not intend carrying incense or pictures of the Virgin back to Wales. Brotherhood is more important than these.

*

It is intended that a preaching and communion service is to be held on the Sunday, according to the liturgy of the French Reformed Church, and it will be led by the parish minister, a Swiss, naturally. There is some concern among us because most of the Anglicans and the occasional Lutheran will not be able take communion with us, in case they go against the discipline of their own communities. This is also true, of course, of the brothers from Orthodox bodies of the East who are with us, and one Old Catholic from Austria. A meeting was held this evening to discuss the issue in order to prevent bitter feelings arising following the service on Sunday morning. My task during the meeting was to explain the meaning of open communion as one who is partial to it, and at the same time to encourage mutual understanding on the subject. I did my best. But I'm afraid that all talk of union where there is no willingness to share communion is empty.

30 July (Saturday)

It fell to me to lead the preparatory service for the communion which is to be held tomorrow: to prepare the majority to participate and a minority to refuse (except 'spiritually'). I hope that I said something that would touch the conscience of those who participated and those who refused.

I certainly touched my own conscience. As I approach the communion table I feel acutely my own guilt and that of the world. I have heard Christians for whom I have the greatest respect saying that they have never had any benefit from a communion service. I expect that the reason for this is that we have made the Eucharist so dissimilar to what it was, that is a meal for brothers and sisters in Christ. The breaking of the bread into small pieces and drinking from dolls' tea party cups and being painfully concerned about the mechanism of the rite has gone far to destroy the naturalness of the act; and it has been my conviction for a long while that the true nature of the Eucharistic meal should be restored, and a natural supper shared with all with thanksgiving. After all, the elements of the Eucharist are elements that sustain our lives, and if we fail to see Christ in tea and sandwiches it is pointless for us to try and see him in artificial crumbs and a thimbleful of red liquid. But despite all of this the Communion, even as it is, places us under the shadow of the Cross, beneath the judgement and grace of the Creator and Lover. That's Him. Ecce Homo[12] – and our corruption vainly attempting to overwhelm him.

31 July (The Lord's Day)

We had the communion – and the non-participation; a service in French led by the local minister, and a sermon in English by an American who could not participate, and I saying in Welsh, as I raised the only cup, 'The cup of blessing for which we give thanks is the communion in the blood of our Lord Jesus Christ, the blood of the New Covenant which was shed for us.' 'Au revoir, mon frére', said the minister to me as we parted. Where will we find that *revoir*, I wonder? 'And so we shall all come together to the oneness in our faith and in our knowledge of the Son of God; we shall become mature people, reaching to the very height of Christ's stature. Then we shall no longer be children, carried by the waves and blown about by every shifting wind of the teaching of deceitful people, who lead others into error by the tricks they invent. Instead, by speaking the truth in a spirit of love, we must grow up to Christ, who is the head. Under his control all the different parts of the body fit together, and the whole body is held together by every joint with which it is provided. So when each separate part works as it should, the whole body grows and builds itself up through love.'[13]

O altitudo divitiarum sapientiae et scientiae Dei![14]

1 August (Monday)

This is the National Day of Switzerland and a great crowd of us went in the evening to the celebration in the nearby village. The audience was small to hear the speeches by local officers and the member of parliament, and the singing of the national anthems was tame and ragged (the longest of them was sung to the tune of 'God save the King'). The themes were the ideals of Switzerland – and there was no inflaming of the assembly either for good or evil. A good number gathered together to enjoy a bonfire on an open space and to delight in the rockets and the fireworks and Catherine wheels. There was not much excitement here either until the ecumenical crowd let themselves go to dance and to sing around the bonfire.

I have a longing for Wales and her incomparable Eisteddfod. Switzerland is a country by itself; Wales is also a country by itself. Every true nation is a chosen nation. I believe that Wales exists because the Providence of the Blessed and Only Ruler insists that it does. And the purpose of its striving and tribulation is this: to bind culture and democracy and peace to the glory of the One who made of one blood every nation of men to dwell throughout the whole earth.

2 August (Tuesday)

Even in the short time I have been here I have been drawn into a kind of network of personal relationships. The likeable, naïve, popular Dutchman; the monkish, secretive Austrian, who led compline in Latin yesterday; the warm-hearted girl from Saarland; the heroic-looking German from Münster; the noble bearded archimandrite from Greece; the dear, gentle, grateful priest-in-training, as faithful as you, from Ethiopia – these and others are part of the pattern of my life now. I will forget them and yet I will never forget them.

There is some loving pain in my heart as I associate with this young selection of the human race. Relating without fully knowing; loving without loving enough – that is the perplexity of our lives this side of the heavenly gates.

Our Father, who knows every one of us, fulfil our lives in one another's lives. For the sake of the Word whom the world did not know. Amen.

3 August (Wednesday)

The idea that I have wronged others pains my heart, that I have grown and developed and found my path at the expense of friends and lovers.

I recall the moral nightmare that came to me in adolescence; a kind of storm of contradictions between puritanism and paganism, between ideal and passion, between affection and friendship and ambition. And my adolescence lasted a long time; I am not sure if it has ended yet.

The worry I have is that the storm that was within me overwhelmed other lives. I remember them, friends for a while, lovers for a while – and accusers for ever. Those were the lives which I touched, and defiled and harmed and disappointed.

Is not every friendship that has died, every empty promise, every barren kiss, a sign of failure and sin? Is it not a component of the curse that it is the will which insists on disregarding tearful cries and entreating arms for the sake of following its own course?

Away, ghosts which I betrayed previously. Every smile and tear of yours is bitter. I immersed my hands in your blood. Was it not violence and murder to show you affection without loving you with the love that will not fail?

4 August (Thursday)

I left the conference late last night and here I am returning on the train through France. It is a pleasure to look homewards. Because of my eagerness the journey seems tedious. I cannot concentrate on anything, nor read nor look at the country nor study my fellow travellers. And the voices and the faces of the past come to disturb me: a screech and groan and abuse, scornful eyes, tight lips, pale cheeks with tears on them.

5 August (Friday)

Having travelled all night, my tired eyes received a blessing from looking at the most beautiful scene I have seen for weeks (yes, although I have been to Switzerland) – a row of elegant, colourful, willowherb flowers against a little lake in beloved Wales. Knowing that my home was near gave a certain extra glow to water and mountain air. This Odysseus is not going to leave Ithaca for some time yet.

CHAPTER 11

TOSSING AND TURNING

6 August (Saturday)

A great deal can be learnt from watching children at play, and there is a place for studying their quarrels. Disagreements when sweets are shared, jealousy of one another, quarrels concerning possessions, temper and childishness – it is striking how similar they are to adults. I noticed that occasional quarrels arise from conflict between will and will; each demanding its own way, each demanding to be uppermost.

I suppose it is possible to divide children into two kinds: those that demand dominion and those who are willing to follow their lead. I noted that some are born leaders before they even start walking. I particularly noticed in watching little girls playing that one would demand to be in charge – or, perhaps, two, and if so the storm will not be far away.

Adults will try to hide the conflict to some degree. But the pulling and pushing exist, nevertheless. In every friendship, in every love, in every movement, in every society, hidden or publicly, there is no end to the battle until the masters are acknowledged as masters – or accept that the battle is in vain.

7 August (The Lord's Day)

Thanks for the opportunity to hear a sermon and thanks for a gripping sermon which drew me closer to Christ.

We were given a picture of Jesus who encourages

and enlightens and convinces and leads. A servant and lord; obedience and sovereignty; self-emptying and self-accomplished – the Person cannot be understood without understanding the Work.

Every Christology is vain which neglects the will of Christ. The books on the history of Christian doctrines in the early centuries usually suggest that the important Christological period ends with the Council of Chalcedon which finally declared the doctrine concerning the Two Natures in Christ, although some praise Leontius of Byzantium[1] for tying the untidy threads of the doctrine together afterwards. Usually the later debate about the will of Christ – whether he had one or two wills – is considered as an unimportant echo of the more famous debate about his nature. This is to misunderstand the subject. In moving the basis of the debate from ontology to teleology, from the world of Being to the world of Will, it became a lot closer to biblical categories and also to the psychological method of understanding the doctrine.

But a diary is not the right place for technical language.

8 August (Monday)

Among the ministers I had the educative experience of knowing there are two whom I shall name 'Tyrannus' and 'Exiguus'. Tyrannus wished to be masterful everywhere. I heard more than one person refer to him as the 'boss'. (It was customary among many women of the 'working class', when I was a boy, to use this word of their husbands. I don't know whether the custom prevails.) He demanded his own way in everything. Opponents could not stay long in his church. The sharpness of his look frightened everyone, and there was a withering coldness in his facetiousness. Everybody bowed or fled before him. Even his smile was icy. How different from Exiguus's smile. He would smile without ceasing. He was a spineless man, prepared to agree with everybody, and he had a foolish habit of finishing your sentences for you to show that he understood you completely and agreed heartily with you. He was wholly devoid of strength, and conviction and loyalty to a cause. His main characteristic, indeed his only one, was niceness. He was the obedient slave of his wife and of everyone else.

'Tyrannus' and 'Exiguus': may both be a warning to us.

I have been accused before now of being both. 'You are as obstinate as a mule. You demand your own way in the end always. You are the boss in your own world, and everyone must yield and bow and conform to your pattern.' On the other hand: 'You are a willing slave to everybody. The world can tread on you, and you do nothing at all but smile weakly. Every lazy fellow can push tasks upon you, and you do nothing but thank them. It's about time you developed a backbone.' Yes: I've heard the two songs from the same voices.

9 August (Tuesday)

The battle between will and will is most passionate when there is the closest relationship between one and the other: two bosom friends seeking the same goal, a man and wife sharing the wonders of sex and life, the saint wrestling with his God.

In the purest friendship there is the purest enmity: in every splendid *amo* there is a frightening *odi*;[2] the hands raised in prayer attempt to grasp the Living God, and force him to listen, to bend, to act.

10 August (Wednesday)

There is a kind of holy war between man and woman. It remains holy despite the work of Strindberg[3] and, to some degree and occasionally, D H Lawrence[4] to de-sanctify it. There *is* a war between the two sexes. Loving a woman is like besieging a castle; and even after an overwhelming victory the question remains which flag flutters on the tower.

11 August (Thursday)

*Oh Powerful Will, who looked at the world to possess it, to lead it, to
    save it;*
*Oh Non-violent Will, who demanded of us, yes, of ourselves, to judge
    that which is righteous;*
Oh Pure Will, who accepted the shame of the Cross;
 Oh Happy Will, who made your home in the Will of the Father;
Guide me, now and for ever.

Yet despite my efforts I cannot feel the Nearness today.

I try to see it with eyes of imagination: calling the fishermen, healing the blind, defeating the demons, challenging the hypocrites, exalting the wretches, declaring the words of Life, cleaning the Temple, disciplining Caesar, dethroning Death.

Oh Authority which neither Creed nor Dogma nor Philosophy can ever tame or imprison!

I have a Great Need. But I feel that the war within me and around me is shaking my foundations.

12 August (Friday)

I had a certain amount of relief today on welcoming McTavish back after spending the most exciting fortnight of his life at the Urdd[5] camp. He returned in a state of happy enthusiasm, singing strange and frightful songs, and his Welsh a little richer and his skin a little browner.

A ten-year-old boy has arrived at some degree of maturity and control which will be smashed before long by the anguish of adolescence. But now the life is enjoying itself like a butterfly in the sunshine. (I have never seen so many butterflies as this year.) And talking of will, *Athanasius contra mundum*![6]

13 August (Saturday)

It is likely that some of Jesus' contemporaries thought that he was stubborn and egocentric. Here is a man who calls men to follow him; here is a man who ventures to give new commandments and principles to the Lord's people and to the people of the world; here is a man who professes to be head of the spiritual world and who strives against unseen powers and human institutions; here is a man who will not listen to the advice of his family nor to the leaders of his society nor even to the warnings of his chief disciple but who turns his face steadfastly towards Jerusalem; here is a man who rejects, even before the court under the threat of crucifixion, any suggestion that he should explain himself to save his life.

Does not the Great Muteness of Jesus suggest some inflexibility, some stubbornness? I wonder whether Caiaphas looked at the Cross and said, 'It's his own fault. I have never seen such obstinacy in a petty Messiah. Suicide: that is what this is.'

But this is the strength of the Utmost Goodness. In the end he must be submitted to or be killed.

And yet he can never be killed; and submitting to him is equal to being fulfilled in him.

14 August (The Lord's Day)

In this excellent sunny weather a man feels that he is a member of the enormous family of *Natura Craetrix*.[7] Sound, sap, sinew, fat, leap and fatigue – that is his habitat. The summer poets describe the colours and forms of the season as if they themselves, the poets, were privileged observers from the outside, sensing the wonders like visitors from another world. But I am compelled by the heat to sense myself and to know myself as a breathless and sweaty animal among the myriads of Nature's children. I expect that the fiery sun has as much pleasure from shining on an acorn or the wing of a hairy caterpillar or the tail of a squirrel as it does in shining on my patient nape.

A sweaty little creature in a meeting house in a small country on an insignificant planet amidst the expansive spaces of the universe saying that the Almighty, Eternal, Awesome Being has visited our planet and has worn his flesh! A little hairy, forked, corpulent body who would not exist except for the heat of the innumerable suns, dares to talk of the Sun of Righteousness and the Light of the World! Here is impudence – but life itself is impudent – and a miracle.

15 August (Monday)

I have been reading *I and Thou* by Martin Buber. Thanks for a philosopher who is closer to a poet than to a champion of technical language. It would be difficult to translate the book into Welsh, since we have no neuter pronoun. The easiest way of overcoming the difficulty is to use 'this thing'. The difference between the personal and the thinginess – if the word 'thinginess' does not exist, it should – is most important in the book. It is a matter of relationship, not of essence. It is a false mysticism which is determined to destroy identity and which drowns every relationship in a sea of nothingness.

16 August (Tuesday)

Buber refers to the 'pretend' playing of children as a proof of the human need for personal relationships. I haven't seen such a surprising example of this than Flanagan's methods of play. She enjoys playing for hours by herself, personalizing every toy or gadget. In the world of imagination where she lives marbles or stones or chalks or pieces of wood become boys and girls and babies. The most entertaining thing is listening to her playing in this way, correcting her children and people or loving them or laughing at them. This is common among children, of course, but I have never seen it before taken to such an extreme extent. Of the two, she would rather tell a story than hear one, and it isn't easy always to distinguish between the factual truth and the poetic truth of some of her more skilful declarations.

Things are not satisfying. We must have persons.

It is better to be slave to a rascal than a slave to a machine.

17 August (Wednesday)

In referring on Saturday to Jesus' inflexibility and stubbornness, it was from the outside that I was looking at his work. To a degree I have recently lost the feeling of his nearness. I tried to meditate about him and regain the old endearing relationship, but my request was too self-conscious to be successful. I fear that I am facing a barren, desert period. But I know from past experiences that Jesus is not inflexible and stubborn for the person who knows and loves him. It is true that no one can weaken his steadfast determination nor turn him away from his saving mission: in this sense he is completely stubborn. But in dealing with a friend, a disciple, a sinner – there is gentleness, patience and mercy. The disciples can bear witness – Peter too quick of tongue and Andrew quiet and humble, Simon the nationalist and Mathew who had been a servant of the Empire, the fiery sons of Zebedee and Thomas who was cautious and questioning.

But oh! I wish I could regain that Lord.

18 August (Thursday)

Around the beginning of the year, when I was able, through some strength which worked on my imagination, to have fellowship with Jesus oftener and more earnestly than at the present, I ventured to write a few devout hymns and poems. Now I am returning to one of these to try and see the Christ afresh by meditating on the vision I had at that time:

> Oh brilliant Love, Oh gentle Breeze
> Which gladdened Galilee,
> Oh generous, uncomplaining sacrifice,
> Which fired old Judea!
>
> You are not far. The pure Breeze
> Will defeat all the centuries,
> And in our lives let Your Fire burn
> Now and for ever.

You did call precious companions,
And they came to follow you;
And you, the Christ, still call
Disciples to follow.

You announced the good Gospel
Of God's goodness and his Kingdom;
To this day you declare the Father,
The Spirit and his fellowship.

You healed the sick and lame and blind,
And in you always there is health,
You plundered the prison house of Satan:
You are our Saviour and Life.

The cross is Your Throne
And the thorns Your pleated Crown.
Your renown fills our hearts,
Our Love and Prince!

Over our barren lives may the breezes
Of Galilee blow;
On the poor altar of our lives
The Fire of Judea will flame.

The lines I wrote a few months back have been a means of
grace to me in my present condition.

I saw him anew, the Eternal Brother, stepping over the
horizons of my world to be beside me.

19 August (Friday)

The great Joy became mine for a little while yesterday, and it
isn't far away today.

*My faithful Brother, who is stronger than death and strife and all
lovelessness, remain with me. Help me to challenge my impurity and
to eradicate it for ever. For in you are the powers and graces of the
incorruptible, infinite Glory. Defend me from myself. Through the
Word and the Cross. Amen.*

20 August (Saturday)

On looking back over the pages of this diary and remembering that it has appeared in a public weekly I am surprised at my boldness. And yet I cannot claim that this journal has been wholly intime. But I have never read an intime journal that has presented the whole truth in all detail. A man's life is bound up with other lives, and recording every thought and posture in my life would break the law concerning libel, treachery and lewdness, without mentioning the pain it would give a kindly editor nor the shock it would give the long-suffering reader.

But I have confessed enough to show how easy and superficial are the confessions of our public prayers. It is so much easier for a man to admit that he is a sinner than to admit that he chews his nails.

21 August (The Lord's Day)

I had supper and conversation with some of the literary notables of Wales and discussed, among other topics, Bohemianism in the literary life of our country. The common assumption is that it is a very uncommon thing in our midst but that it belongs closely, nevertheless, to creative genius and deserves a wondrous tolerance, if not something greater, from the slaves of respectability.

I wonder?

The person who rebels against the unworthy and inhibiting conventions for the sake of enriching and exalting life must be admired; but I have no respect at all for some of the compulsions which occasion a rejection of the habits of our contemporaries. Some try to feed their own vanity by living differently from their neighbours, and they are not much better than ostentatious people preening themselves within the conventions. Others attempt to break small moralities in order to be able to savour publicity: there is a market for Bohemianism by now. The aim of some is to try to satisfy their consciences by challenging society in the insignificant things, and they know in their hearts that they are wholly servile to society in the more important matters. It is easier to wear a yellow shirt at a funeral than to support peace in a time of war.

Fair play. One has to admit that the occasional Bohemian is a rebel by nature or from principle – in the small things and the great things. The flag of freedom and justice and humanity is the massive dicky bow that is worn by him. His life is a protest against stupid uniformity which demands the subjection of every passion and every talent and every conscience beneath the paw of the Beast. All praise to him; but perhaps his protest would be more effective if his dicky bow was a little smaller.

Society must be challenged so that it can be saved: not challenged for its own sake. And giving to the insignificant details the importance which belongs to the great principles must be avoided.

And incidentally: is it not unfair to use the word 'Bohemianism' to give a Romantic shine to deceit and fraud and fickleness and dipsomania and nymphomania? We need to be saved from the pharisaism of the synagogue and the salon alike.

*

I received two favours from one of the notables this evening, a criticism of my sermon ('pills in sugar') and the loan of a book, the diary of Barbellion, *The Journal of a Disappointed Man*.[8]

22 August (Monday)

As I travelled home my thoughts were clouded by the memory of a nasty nightmare I had last night, which was a dream that I arrived at my home and found Flanagan and Ap Siencyn dead. It is true that they revived miraculously by the end of my dream, but I am still trembling.

Phosphorous in the frightening darkness – that is human life – but it bears witness to the Sun of suns.

23 August (Tuesday)

An old friend of Taranwen came for a day or two, bringing her two children with her and a little niece who helps with the task of caring for the little ones. It is interesting to get a glimpse of the worries and hopes of another family.

'Is not this the carpenter, the son of Mary, and the brother of James, Joseph, and Judas and Simon? Are not his sisters living here?'[9]

I was invited in by my young friend Jesus – some years younger than I was acquainted with, but as I gazed at the keen bright eyes I noticed a scar already there. There was life in his smile and speech; as I rejoiced in him I felt that it was superb for me that I was able to breathe air and to sense the world.

I followed him into the workshop and saw the lads: James, a well-built, good-looking young man, slow of movement, and his love of his older brother to be seen in the eyes which looked on him with admiration; Joseph was a lively, mischievous, talkative boy with a striking likeness to Jesus in his looks; Judas and Simon the two playful boys around ten-years-old, the first as persistent as the other was fickle. They were talking nineteen to the dozen, everyone except James. He was handling a piece of wood with a knife, and Joseph was giving him jocular counsel. Suddenly there was a scream from the corner where Simon had been imitating one of the important officials of the synagogue; Judas was trying to teach him some respect by giving him a clout with a big spoon.

I looked from one to the other. They were Brothers of the Lord, the children of Mary and Joseph. They were part of the Incarnation, and if these, what about John the Baptist as well, and Mary Magdalene? – and Herod and Caiaphas – and King David and Dafydd ap Gwilym – and Hammurabi and Savonarola and Henry Ford?[10] – and the Brother of Low Degree? We are all part of the Incarnation.

I heard female voices outside the door. Mary and her girls were coming.

No. It was Flanagan saying that tea was ready.

24 August (Wednesday)

We say goodbye to McTavish for another week or so. He is going to stay in the Rhondda at the home of his friend Rhiwallon.

I have been reading Amiel's[11] diary recently, reading it in bed before going to sleep; it is a book to be sipped, its taste being mystical and permanent. Barbellion insists on reading it from beginning to end at one sitting. I pity him, with his thirst for praise and his fears and his weakness and his cleverness and his liveliness and his interests in live animals. He is stronger and weaker than I at about the same age. Amiel also deserves our pity; but his thinking deserves solemn respect, and his social comprehension is remarkably relevant, occasionally, to the twentieth century.

25 August (Thursday)

My young Fellow man, who was so generous until the oppressive world killed you, my gratitude is boundless that you can never be killed and that you are still able to savour fresh air and the fair light of the Resurrection morning. Lead my soul along the paths of truth. Cause me to know myself in you. I have not yet dared to look at the slime of my loathing. Sustain me with your smile and tear.

26 August (Friday)

Occasionally, when I put the children to bed, I hear snatches of Beethoven's violin concerto, and painful memories come to trouble me. Such divine skill on such earthly simplicity! I remember hearing this marvel for the first time, before I dreamt of being a father.

27 August (Saturday)

The newspapers make me sick these days. Usually, the political news – despite, with few exceptions, their revulsion – is an escape from the daily pageant of crime and vulgarity. But at the present, the conflict between national aspirations and imperial pride is more prominent, and with the pride there is, from the viewpoint of the Western Powers, a great deal of cowardly militarism which dares not allow Cypriot and Moroccan to endanger their military 'safety'.[12] But the situation is presented with the presupposition that it is beneficial in the present tension between Communism and the West to retain as much power as possible in the hands of France and England and that their subjects in Morocco and Cyprus should not be too discontented. Greed and violence and crime are the oppressions of the enemy; 'our' oppression is beneficent defence: the old, old story. But the trouble is not only recognizing the deceit but thinking of the millions in many countries who are conditioned to accept it.

*

But here is a happier topic: a young man and his girl pay us a visit, one to stay the night and the other for a few days, one from Gwynedd and the other from Germany. The vivacity of adolescence is lively, fresh and sparkling. I recall that I began longing for my lost youth when I reached twenty years of age. But, good gracious, I haven't completely lost it yet.

28 August (The Lord's Day)

It is encouraging to be able to enjoy Sunday in the company of a genial fellow minister.

Occasionally during the work of the day I felt that my head was leaning on the eternal Gentleness as if on his breast.

I felt at other times that someone or something was arguing against me and accusing me before the Eternal.

This is Satan in the Book of Job: the prosecutor attempting to revile the righteous before God.

But this time my great worry is that the Righteous One is the Accuser.

29 August (Monday)

I saw him again in his beauty, my Jesus, my Heavenly Brother, King of Mankind. He was the Life of the Universe. The Glory and Beauty of Creation. His smile was like the dawn and his look was like the sun in its strength, his speech like a river winding between fertile meadows, and his whole person excelled over the splendour of mountain and sea. He was the Anointed One. His was the Kingdom and the Victory.

The scars of his suffering shone like dark bright stars in the majestic firmament of his beauty.

In him there was an unutterable strength which drew me towards him. His life was possessing my life, his endless tenderness was compelling me, his unyielding heroism attracted and mastered me.

Suddenly I experienced the heavenly captivity as shameful and insulting. I struggled to free myself. I was not going to be a subject or a disciple to anyone or anything. I tried to revolt against the oppressive tyranny of the Omnipresent Love. A flame rose in my breast, a flame of protest against the Exalted One.

And I, in the form of a Man, did not think it wrong to be equal to God.

I felt that I was being drawn unmercifully towards the Eternal Mercy. I saw the loveable Face coming closer and my Reality melting into the Reality of the Blessed One.

Suddenly the flame in my breast broke and spread until my life was turned into a hell of murderous anger, and I know that I made a gesture of striking.

'Who hit you? Guess!'

'Why do you hit me?'[13]

*

Why have I taken so long to confess my deepest sin? It is Lucifer's sin.

No: that description gives it too much dignity. The sin of Cain, rather. No: there is pride in that claim also. I know what my sin is: my voice is that last voice, that terrible day in Palestine long ago, which was raised in a weakly, shaky, deadly scream, to shout 'Crucify him'.

30 August (Tuesday)

I have been vainly searching for words to pray. There is some tumult within me where peace ought to be.

31 August (Wednesday)

It was sad for us to say goodbye to Thrinchen. She had opened her petals for us before the end of her short stay with us. But McTavish returns, and Rhiwallon with him to stay here for the rest of the week. And in the company of Arfon, a new lad who has come to live near us, how the two throw themselves into play, as if there were no tumults anywhere in the world, neither in Morocco nor in my heart. Such happiness seems to me today to be incredible.

1 September (Thursday)

When the spear-armed forces of hell attack a man's soul, they conquer everything.

*

I noticed on reading diaries written by others who had no intention of publishing them (not immediately, at any rate) that the dairy sometimes becomes a kind of friend to its author. On its white breast the diarist, even in his severest loneliness, receives a resting place and a release. In front of his secretive and safe friend he can pour out the mysteries of his experience.

This diary is not a friend but an enemy. Writing it, at the

moment, is a kind of purgatory. But what value is there in a confession book which is kept from my contemporaries? Does not a confession cease to be confession if it is kept secret? It is not sufficient to take my sin to God in secret: he is well aware of it already. It is painful to shed all the multi-coloured attire of hypocrisy, but it must be done – even when hypocrisy masquerades as decency.

*

The forces of hell are a block on my soul, my home, my country, my world, and I do not know how to act. At this moment I must choose. Should I commit a betrayal here to save my soul over there? Should I give up one duty in order to be faithful in another duty and to bring succour to a poor wretch whose claim on me is so importunate and inevitable?

My God, my God, direct me, support me. The Good Shepherd, fetch your lost sheep. Come to me amidst the vast spaces of the wilderness.

Every member of our little family has his own special tune. This was decided many years ago, and there is much benefit and happiness in this folly. Taranwen's tune is 'He will feed His sheep' from Handel's *Messiah*. The heart-soothing beauty of the tune comes to comfort me today as a breeze from paradise.

2 September (Friday)

is missing from the original edition

3 September (Saturday)

I escorted Anna to my sister Phyllis's house and left her there to keep a church appointment.[14]

*

We had some difficulty to nurse McTavish during the first months of his life, and we were fearful that we might lose him. At that time, I used to try and ease him by singing 'Morfa Rhuddlan',[15] not the old tune but the other, and in our family now the heartbreaking beauty of the tune belongs especially to McTavish. After that, we gave tunes to other members of the family. Handel's 'He will feed his sheep' is Taranwen's tune; I was given the splendid tune, 'Saint Anthony's Chorale', which Brahms composed with brilliant variations. Flanagan received a little tune from Germany, 'In einem kühlen Grunde', whose beauty transforms even heartbreak into pure heaven, and Ap Siencyn the delightful second movement of Beethoven's *Pastoral Symphony* – I swear that it suits him down to the ground. And when Anna came to live with us she had to be given a tune as well – the well-known theme in the largo in Dvorak's *New World Symphony*.

There is glory in all the tunes, glory and passion and charm. They testify, somehow, to the relationship that should exist between us, and the unity in diversity which is one of the basic principles of the Creation. And when I am tempted to doubt the relationship, they come to strengthen me in the love which, despite every storm, holds us together.

4 September (The Lord's Day)

I preached about the human relationships which are so valuable to all of us and for the need to gather them together, transform them and to unite them in the privileged Relationship which was portrayed for us in the Anointed One.

But the Grace which I preached turned into a judgement on myself.

5 September (Monday)

It is strange saying goodbye to Rhiwallon. His quiet likeableness is quite different from the various kinds of cacophony and indiscipline which we have become used to in our family.

Our old friend Felicia comes to stay with us, full of energy and organizing talent and goodwill as usual. It is quite interesting hearing her stories: Anita had become a Roman Catholic (and she had been a Methodist and a Baptist and nearly a Quaker); Mrs Mortimer dominated her grandchild in a selfish possessiveness; Montagu was thinking of leaving the ministry to serve in the civil service.

I realized afresh how complicated is the relationship even between two. A man's goodness can become a burden to his best friend.

*

My predicament is still with me. One must choose between fidelity to a cause and mercy towards a dear one whose life is so near to my life. It is a growing nightmare.

6 September (Tuesday)

I saw the Gloriousness like a Sun above my head. It ran across the sky and hovered and turned and fell. It fell upon me. I could only see never-ending light, as if a sea of light had drowned the whole earth. Glory to God in the highest... Shepherds, wise men, the oxen and the ass, a baby crying, a mother musing – no phenomenon has ever been so cherished.

I became conscious of the Spirit moving on the surface of the waters, and in the tumultuous mist there came a point of incredible light. I hid in it, for this was my home and destiny and my whole world. I suddenly felt that I was part of an explosion of sparks, but before long I was wandering among suns and vast spaces and marvels. I was a planet, and then a cloud and after that a drop of water. I trembled and shivered. I began striving and struggling. I swam, became swollen, I dragged along, and the Wind blew through my bowels and my being. I grew, I propagated, I multiplied. The pageantry and pomp of the species moved around me. I revealed a lust and emotion in claw and violent tooth and manic skirmishes. I learnt to socialize and to communicate. I made weapons and homes and cemeteries. I raised a tower, and laughed in the abundance of my strength and arrogance and wept in the agonies of my failures. Loving and hating, being jealous and ashamed, breaking a promise and breaking a heart, mocking and sighing – a multitude of agonies and pleasures came to me. I dreamt of angels and glories. I sacrificed and I bowed down. The Wind caught me and shook me. I wrestled with invisible mercies in terror and longing and great love.

Night befell me and in the night I heard the cry of the baby. A Little Man had been born, and there was wonderment in his mother's eyes, and the Stars of the Morning greeted the Star which greatly excelled their gentle splendour.

The Word was made flesh because the flesh had been made complete by the Spirit.

Loving beauty and because of that hating the Rose of Sharon and the Lily of the Valley; worshipping the Truth and, in the passion of the worship, spitting on the Son of Truth; craving the Utmost Goodness and because of the insatiability of the lust, screaming murderously against the Firstborn of the Eternal Goodness – this is my calamity and destruction.

7 September (Wednesday)

I succeeded in relaxing a little today. The children went back to school yesterday and Felicia and Taranwen and I have a chance to go for a walk in the country and become antiquarians and naturalists for the sunnier part of the day. We went to Tretower and appreciated the old tower and the old house, and it was a pleasure to see the swallows congregating before emigrating. What fun and joy in the sunshine. There they are on the church roof flying around in circles and chattering like a women's meeting enjoying a cup of tea.

We enjoyed ourselves, but in all enjoyment there is some suggestion of deceit and of pretence. The paint of the clown is on our faces and the hum of destruction is in our hearts.

8 September (Thursday)

I took the children to their school bus this morning, and had great fun – observing a spider's web between the wires in the railway's boundary, and the dew like pearls on the thin strands; and then, of course, seeing hundreds of webs on the hedge and the adjacent trees. Artistry, technology, enterprise: the spider knows something about all of them.

It is a pity that cruelty towards the males is such a distinct characteristic among the females in the world of the spider: the war between the sexes is a fairly ancient war; and there is no talk of a peace agreement yet.

*

The beauty of the volcano against the blue sky is unbeatable. The villagers around it believe that it is quiet if not dead, but there is pandemonium in its bowels.

*

Thank you, oh Lord, for the discipline of nature and history and conscience. Discipline me. Do not allow me to expire in disorder. Soothe me, straighten and refine and instruct my soul. Through my Pattern and my Way. Amen.

9 September (Friday)

There is an exciting line in a hymn which says that sin is on fire. What does it mean?

CHAPTER 12

ANGER

10 September (Saturday)

Cardod Pugh called to see me – to plunder my spirit and to sunbathe in my ready admiration. Many times throughout the year he has sucked the blood of my imagination and thought, but I never before experienced so much disgust and impatience and anger as I experienced today.

Confessing the sins of other people has no place at all in this diary – or else writing it would be the greatest of pleasures – and its length would be much more. I have said enough. I will only add that this is an example of a one-sided friendship, if such a thing can be imagined, the one receiving and the other giving, the one pressing and the other groaning, the one enriching and fulfilling himself and the other impoverishing and emptying himself.

Is there friendship between a flea and a dog?

I am full of anger when I see another life fattening so shamefully on my life. There is more than one kind of theft. I find it difficult to forgive someone who steals the fruits of thought and imagination and meditation from me without giving anything. I exist for his sake – that is the presupposition that hides behind every smile and gesture and blather of his.

And yet I gave him everything which he asked for, and much more. And in my heart, the anger still burns.

11 September (The Lord's Day)

I dared to preach, with the imperfection and impropriety of my life and the relationship like lead in my heart.

I supposed at first that the diary would help me to grow in grace; but until now it has only lifted the lid on the cauldron of my devilish nature.

*

I received some comfort later, away from home, in the house of Adelheid and Powys. His brother Lemwel was there, as witty, as lively and as respectful/disrespectful as ever. A minute in his company always turns a tragedy into a comedy.

Adelheid enjoyed it all enormously, looking at us from time to time as if she could see through us. It did my heart good to hear Rolff and Thydain laughing so naturally at their uncle's humour.

12 September (Monday)

What a wonderful hymn is:

> Lord Jesus, lead my soul
> To the Rock which towers over me.[1]

And that is a word of warning to the atomic age. I was disturbed when I read it in the booklet *Emynau'n Gwlad*. I turned then to one of Morgan Rhys' masterpieces, 'Oh open my eyes to see' – and stood on the rock this time to observe the King conquering the offspring of the Devil.

In the hymn it is the 'Offspring of the dragon' that is given. And this is one of the clumsy turns in the history of Wales. A dragon is the most famous symbol of our nationality, but in the wealth of hymns which arose out of the evangelical revival which did so much to save our nation and language, the symbol of the dragon is used time after time to represent the ferocity of the Evil One.

The red dragon is found on a symbolic shield of a Christian institution in Wales and a little time back some people wished to delete it, on the basis that it was symbolic of God's Enemy. The dragon was successfully saved by the efforts of its friends showing that it stood with its head lowered to the ground and that it was therefore submitting to the Almighty.

The truth is that the dragon is a winged serpent and that it has in the Bible itself a beneficent significance. The serpent sometimes signifies salvation and the divine life.

The fact that Saint George, the conqueror of the dragon, is the patron saint of England adds a perfect gem to the confusion. It is the dragon of the Apocalypse that we have here, of course, and it is comforting for us to look occasionally on a small picture on one of the walls in our home, a copy of a picture in an old Flemish hour book, a picture that shows Saint George not having killed the dragon but tamed it. Something similar is seen in the hymn 'Good news has come to our land'.

> All our enemies are now
> In chains to the King almighty.[2]

To the extent that the dragon represents the civilization of man (with reference to the Roman Empire), it is more compatible with the Good News that it be tamed than killed: tamed and disciplined and saved.

Like Origen[3] I look forward to the conversion of the Evil One. In the meantime, let the red dragon give inspiration!

13 September (Tuesday)

I had to yield.

Oh Blessed Mercy, forgive me. Save me from thinking that failure and crime are easy to forgive when the circumstances give a shadow of an excuse and the consequences seem unimportant. I know that I have a part in every betrayal which has corrupted our human lives and in the immense betrayal of the crucifixion of the Righteous One. Forgive me. Save my dear ones, save Wales, save the race. Through the One Who Prayed on the Cross. Amen.

I have nothing to tell you today my Dairy, my Accuser, my Satan. The whiteness of your paper is like the white of the eyes of godly devils.

Eyes: the burning eyes of Judas, Pilate's sullen eyes, the vulture-like eyes of Caiaphas – and the tears in the eyes of Peter in the weak light of daybreak.

14 September (Wednesday)

is missing from the original edition

15 September (Thursday)

All anger towards Cardod Pugh has now disappeared. But his personality remains a mystery to me: his talent, his ambition, his persistence, his morality – and his coldness and his apartness and his mental toughness.

16 September (Friday)

I am too cross with myself to be cross with anyone else.

My only excuse is that I heard the Wolf howling at the door; and to send the Wolf away I had to throw at it the torches of the marriage feast of the ladies who demand the service of every valiant knight.

*

When I think sometimes of our children's pedigree I begin to fear that lycanthropy will come upon them.[4]

*

Perhaps some would be surprised to hear that I am able to sin through anger – since I never lose my temper violently, never lose self-control, never become enraged. Only once do I remember completely losing my self-control and getting into a towering rage. I was a school boy of about twelve at that time; a bully had gone too far. After the madness had passed, the fear returned. Apart from this I have been so tranquil as to be described as a cushion, something soft for the world to sit upon. But there are different kinds of anger. Much of my anger hides behind a smile. 'Whoever is angry with his brother will be brought to trial. But now I tell you whoever calls his brother "You good-for-nothing" will be brought before the Council, and whoever calls his brother a worthless fool will be in danger of going into the fire of hell.'[5]

17 September (Saturday)

I might as well face the analysis of hatred which is found in *Yn y Llyvyr hwnn:* enmity, disunity, strife, arrogance, intolerance, insolence, treachery, malevolence, rage, tumult, evil nature, murder.

Hatred as a state of the soul is meant by 'enmity' and 'treachery' and 'malevolence' and 'evil nature'. 'Strife' and 'arrogance' and 'insolence' signify bickering and quarrelling with words. 'Disunity' implies quarrelling with a friend. Mental madness is implied by 'intolerance'. By 'rage' is meant extreme wrath. These conditions can lead to 'tumult' and to 'murder', which is to kill.

I do not quarrel a lot. To a great extent I have been able to renounce the outward signs of anger. Infrequently have I been guilty of tumult, indeed I do not ever throw myself voluntarily into tumult. I have never committed murder as the term is legally defined. It is rarely that I quarrel with words, although a man has to defend himself sometimes. If my tongue was more flexible it is probable that my transgressions would be more frequent.

But it is not enough to reject outward signs of anger while its fire and brimstone turn the heart into hell. Enmity, malevolence, intolerance – oh that I could escape these into the Love which breathed life into my nostrils.

18 September (The Lord's Day)

I saw her passing as I was preaching in the morning, arm in arm with the arrogant man who had bought her body. I felt sick as I noted the glitter of her bracelets and saw the jewels dancing beneath her ears, as I noticed the paint which covered the dirt and the perfume which mixed with the stench. I heard her sickly laugh change into a screech as her arrogant master pawed her body. I felt contempt, surfeit, disgust. In her resided all the ugliness of our generation. The loathing remained in my heart even as I preached about the forgiveness and love of God.

'Plead with her to stop her adultery and prostitution. If she does not, I will strip her as naked as the day she was born. I will make her like a dry and barren land, and she will die of thirst.'[6]

I saw her again in the evening service, and the dawn on her face, and the surprise in her eyes, and her arms trying to embrace the Intangible.

'*Noli me tangere.*' 'Because I have not yet gone up to my Father.'[7]

19 September (Monday)

I had to attend committees today, and I groaned together with my fellow ministers.

I was on the verge of buying a copy of the *Cyfansoddiadau a Beirniadaethau*[8] of Pwllheli – could not a more convenient title be found for the annual publication of the National Eisteddfod, by the way? – but one of the kindest hearts in Wales pities me, and I receive the valuable volume as a gift.

I read the winning short story with enjoyment after realizing that it was much better than the promise of the opening paragraphs.

'No one ever organizes anything. There is no need to organize. It is *different* here John... It is from inward compulsions that we do things. We are free from the oppression of committees and councils and organizations.'

The storyteller suggests that it is so in heaven. But what is the meaning of the Welsh proverb: 'Hell needs only to be organized'?

20 September (Tuesday)

Years ago, before I finally turned to the Incarnate One, a violent and distasteful misanthropy was a permanent part of my behaviour. It faded under the rays of the Sun, leaving only an outline rim of ludicrous cynicism. I fear that the old misanthropy is now returning.

Does not mankind deserve every contempt? Here they are, the privileged members of the Honourable Society of the Live Creatures, participants of the peerless enterprise of Creation, brothers and sisters of the Son of Prophecy, builders of houses and temples and the towers of the Glittering City – and yet there is a stench in their souls which is much more hateful than the stench of the slime from which they crawled. The need and crisis of Man ask a sacrifice from us – but men will only lust in craving for knowledge of the personal history of some actress or princess. The scientists are experimenting with the fabric of creation and the states gather bombs of destruction – and men will only gamble on the football pools and go on strike not for justice but for better wages than their fellow workers. Great wonders have been achieved in inventions and knowledge and civilization – and men will only stare at the shoddiest things on the television screen. The Christs lie in their blood – and men will only scratch for gold and pour a considerable amount of it into the pockets of the pseudo-aristocrats who know how to lead civilization to destruction and entertain the fatheads on the broad way towards it.

It was knowledge, skill and cleverness that built the Tower of Babel and every masterpiece of civilization which the world ever saw. But their debris is witness to the stupidity and clumsiness and ignorance of man. Hankering after magical fruits and bypassing the Tree of Life – that has always been the history of man. And there has never been a better example of this buffoonery than man's pranks in the twentieth century.

And if the final destruction comes to humankind, will the event be more important in the motion of the immense spheres than the death of the smallest insect under the heel of stupid man?

Is it possible to respect such a mob of scoundrels and louts as the human race? Is it possible to love without respecting? But are mockery and hatred the only things which humankind deserve, and the only things that a sensible and conscientious man can give to it?

'For God loved the world so much.'[9] Where was the self-respect of the Ancient of Days?

> Oh Lord Jesus, who forgave even the Cross, forgive the hell that burns in my heart. Let me see the humanity which was destined for us, the wounds so brilliant and worthy on Your body, and all the glory of nature a crown on Your head, and the Flesh which had been an abode for the Word rising in front of me in the abundance of his beauty and strength. Give me Your Own Self, the Man who Declares God, now and forever.

21 September (Wednesday)

Rhiwallon comes to stay with us for a few days, all smiles. It is not so difficult to love mankind today.

I went happily to preach with the Baptists and received a fulsome welcome, and was conveyed home by car by a Good Samaritan.

22 September (Thursday)

A sense of humour is a considerable help in surviving ordination services.

A blessing be upon the young minister. May the Spirit lead him past every obscurantism and false gospel to the Truth. There are plenty of swamps and mud on his path.

In the Church itself there is plenty to feed misanthropy:

kneeling or bowing the head before the great Freeman, and enthroning an institution or agency or movement in his stead; praising his grace and peace and agreeing to kill his family; kissing and betraying him as happened before many times.

23 September (Friday)

As my misanthropy grows I meet with Cardod Pugh. Martial's epigram about Sabidius comes to mind.[10]

24 September (Saturday)

Some claim that ministers are poor listeners. Their tendency, it is said, is to plan sermons on the text themselves instead of listening to the preacher; or if they listen, they listen critically and not as sinners. But this is not true of most of them, especially at festivals. They accept their medicine in a brotherly and gentle spirit.

And there are the warm-hearted Welsh in London. After the welcome I received it is rather difficult to believe in my own misanthropy. My malaise has disappeared. The bitter hatreds that have been choking and defiling my spirit recently have come to an end. Hating humankind, hating the immaculate Love himself – my life has gone astray in disgust similar to one of the London fogs. But here, among the Welsh who are away from home, in London itself, there is pleasure once more in fellowship and in worship.

25 September (The Lord's Day)

It was of great encouragement to receive generous assurance today that publishing this revealing diary week by week has not been in vain. It is obvious that some persons have followed these confessions and seen in them something of psychological interest. I have been fearful more than once that this tiresome journey has been taxing for saints and sinners alike. Examining my sin has been a longer and more costly undertaking than I expected. I have not finished yet and I am not certain whether I will have the release that I am longing for. But I feel – today at least – that I am a more honest man than I was nine months ago.

But have I expelled the Christ from my heart?

> He is ready to make his home
> In the black, guilty heart,
> And to beautify it with the graces,
> The precious gifts of heaven above.[11]

God in Christ, Christ in the fellowship of his saints, the fellowship of the saints in God – those were my topics today. May the Sun shine in my own heart.

26 September (Monday)

I had to hurry home to my work. On the way, I tried to delete all lovelessness from my breast: the secret reviling which has been gnawing me inwardly, the tendency to judge my contemporaries by their faults alone, the lack of patience in the face of other people's self-interest, the habit of classifying a man's character on the first meeting and refusing to believe that he could be better than my ungraceful verdict.

> *The Christ, the Eternal Son, the Abiding Brother, the One who Endured Suffering and Pain, forgive me. Heal my soul, cleanse my lips. Do not allow me to mock the despicable men because they are unlike the Man. Give me the forgiving love of the Cross, now and every hour of my life!*

27 September (Tuesday)

To what extent am I guilty of that sneaky sin, talking maliciously of other people's faults behind their backs?

There is more than one kind of gossip: discussing our neighbours' weaknesses and follies and better qualities out of fun or enjoyment; complaining about some in a manner which gives expression to disfavour; mocking or reviling a fellow sinner maliciously or hatefully. It is easy to plead guilty to the first transgression, if it is indeed a transgression. One of the happiest privileges of life is to enjoy one another's peculiarities; it is pleasant in the company of a genial friend to discuss our neighbours' peccadillos and note in fun on the mote and indeed the occasional beam in a brother's eye. The pity is that it is a lot more difficult to have the same enjoyment at one another's expense in one another's presence. I know a man who enjoys giving pleasure in company by imitating speech impediment and lameness. How easily and how unaware does politeness become hypocrisy and kindness deceit.

I am also guilty sometimes of the second kind of gossip: grumbling, complaining, expressing contempt and disgust, agreeing with my fellow critics that so-and-so is a big baby, and that she is the greatest telltale in the country; that Dick is a soulless, conceited fellow, that Siôn is two-faced, that Dafydd is too big for his boots, and that their wives in the same order, are a flirt, a churl and a fat chatterbox. It is difficult to decide where the first kind of gossip, which is quite harmless, ends, and where the second, which is a danger to a man's soul, begins.

But there is a third kind of gossip: the loathsome and poisonous maligning, the bilious and murderous scourging, the killing with the tongue.

Has my tongue ever tasted my neighbour's blood?

*

I wonder whether it is possible to kill not only with the tongue but also with the mind?

28 September (Wednesday)

One of my past losses came to visit my imagination and I was unsuccessful in closing the door in its face. Perhaps it was an evil spirit, but it had the complexion and appearance of someone I loved and whom I had lost.

'You desired death', she said.

'No', I answered.

'Don't deny it', she said. 'That fair afternoon, when you were saying farewell, smiling gently at me and shaking my hand, you wished my death.'

'Don't frighten me', I said. 'Even if it were true it would not be unusual. Many, from time to time, desire death to others. I am sure there is no one in the world whose death someone somewhere has not desired.'

'You are hiding behind the sin of mankind. The desire came into your mind that afternoon, as you said farewell, with the white clouds suspended in the sky and in the depth of the lake.'

'No, friend. It was a transient shadow that was on the surface of the lake, and the edge of a cloud soothed the great heat of the sun.'

'It was a shadow on your heart.'

'It was a desire for my own death.'

'It is your own death that you are desiring now.'

She withdrew, and her withdrawal took away the beauty of the day.

29 September (Thursday)

The business of the week reached its apex today; and thank goodness for that.

After tea, Rhiwallon and McTavish and Flanagan enjoyed a moment of pretend play. And it was terrifying play – playing lepers, lifting their arms and shouting 'Unclean! Unclean!' – and then laughing and forgetting.

The fair visor fell for a moment as it were, and revealed the skull.

30 September (Friday)

I mused about all the agonies and losses of mankind: the breaking of agreements and the breaking of hearts, disease and scurvy, madness and mourning, sighing and screeching and the silence of death. It was as if there was a world of technicians and engineers under the leadership of a mad arch scientist attacking the earth's inhabitants with all kinds of imprisoning and destructive weapons, attacking soul and mind and body, and the hermit in his cell and the baby in its cradle and the ruler on his throne. A strange anger came over me, a joyful, victorious anger, and I suddenly felt that I was with Jesus and that I had within me the same anger that he had within him. 'A man suffering from leprosy came to Jesus, knelt down, and begged him for help, "If you want to," he said, "you can make me clean." Jesus was filled with pity, and stretched out his hand and touched him. "I do want to", he answered. "Be clean."'

An early reading of this passage from the first chapter of Mark has 'with anger' and not 'with pity'. It is the anger of compassion, anger at evil, flaming with glorious courage and comeliness against the powers that deprive and torture men.

1 October (Saturday)

Oh Christ, my Prophet, my Priest, my King, sanctify every anger which is within me with Your Own Anger. Burn in me, the eternal Fire, until every impurity and every destructive hate is demolished. Burn within me the sacrificial Flame, and burn within us all until the earth is sanctified, until man is deified. Draw us to you, Oh Dweller of the Bush, Oh Monarch of the White, Brilliant Throne, draw us to the heart of the Fire of Your Mercy now and for ever. Amen.

'And suddenly…' That is the glory of Mark's Gospel: it makes us see the fire of the battle between the pure wrath of the Anointed One and the mad hatred of the Evil One.

2 October (The Lord's Day)

I was enabled to preach today in a chapel in Monmouthshire, in one of the most easterly of Welsh-language churches in Wales, on one of the heights which still manages to rise above the flood of English which has flooded the county. I was able to taste the 'the tears of things,' and the taste was bitter. But the charming inheritance of an ordinary worshipping people remains agreeable still.

What is Providence but election? Was not every nation elected to enrich the treasury of the submissive Grace? And was not Wales elected to the Great Partnership? We must beware of betraying the election.

3 October (Monday)

Harvest thanksgiving services are one of the great attractions in this county. A multitude of people put in an appearance who do not attend during the year. These are the rice Christians. God is a millionaire in their view, and the purpose of the harvest festival is to gain his protection with a little flattery; the ten-shilling note is a spoon to gain a ladle. The custom is old, older than the offering of the Silurian of old to Amaethon, or whoever was the god of crops.

But the agricultural festival is an opportunity, every time it comes, to praise the Seed of Woman; but to some, however, the God of Nature is the same as the God of Grace.

As I went to preach to a place where the court of the princes of Breconshire was held at one time, it was natural to think of the ancient worshippers of Wales. The ages march past, but need and mercy remain.

I preached God's love, the Love which creates life – and creates love.

God is love. In him there is no hatred. His wrath is not his hatred.

I tried to imagine the God who would be furious and mad: I tried to perceive the frightening infinity falling upon me to punish and destroy me: I saw it, the beast of Judgement terrifying my soul: tooth and claw, roar and surge above my head. I failed to perceive more. The compass of my imagination is hopelessly limited. And I refused to believe. The Beast of Terror above my head was not God. It was God's enemy.

What is the wrath of God? Not a God who is offended

like a finite man with his limited spiritual assets. Rejecting all lovelessness – that is the wrath of God. And for the divine wrath which man experiences in history, we must accept the interpretation of Dodd in his commentary on Romans. That is the loving order which has given us life and will and freedom to choose and has ensured that evil is evil, that an offence is destructive and a transgression is poisonous because goodness is creative and rightness is health-giving. That is the order of providence, and we must be grateful for it.

If all suffering were exiled from the whole world there would only remain a vast cemetery, quiet and dark.

'For the wrath of God was revealed from heaven against all the sin and evil of men.'[12]

'And the same is true of what God has done. He wanted to show his wrath and to make his power known. But he was very patient in enduring those who were the objects of his wrath, who were doomed to destruction.'[13]

It is not a God who takes offence who is here but God longing for us in patience and mercy and with long suffering. Wrath is only a good providence which ensures failure to the unclean until he is cleansed. It is to demean God to suppose that he can lose patience and strike. The wrath that Paul discusses belongs to the order of the world and not to the heart of the Creator.

4 October (Tuesday)

I throw myself into the work of a new term and I thank God for the privileges.

As I shared the bread and wine I felt that my hands did not belong to me. Despite all unnaturalness and every error the communion brings us fearfully close to Jesus – to the betrayal and tyranny and failure and corruption of his enemies and friends and to the humanity and godliness of the Broken Heart and the Wrath which has been struggling with evil.

It is not enough, after all, to explain the wrath of God as the impersonal principle that 'sin pays a wage, and the wage is death'. There is a personal wrath as well (or the ultra-personal: I say 'personal' because our minds cannot grasp the Ultra-person). But this kind of divine wrath cannot be understood without considering the wrath of Christ and the saints. The wrath of God is the same as the wrath of Jesus. The graceful wrath flashed and flamed from the beginning of history until now. It burnt in the hearts of God's prophets and missionaries and it conquered the fortresses of corruption and anger. We would have no hope without it.

5 October (Wednesday)

Today a class under my care started in one of the industrial valleys, a class on the religious and social history of Wales. It will be quite interesting noting the discussions from week to week, for the membership represents the more intelligent levels of the population quite well.

I am amazed at the power and might of Christ in Michelangelo's *Great Judgement*. As I meditate about him I see him approaching me gradually and his face changing until I see, not Michelangelo's Christ, but the amazing Christ by Rembrandt, the Jesus who has always been dear to me, the Jesus who is the foundation of the picture of him that I have in my imagination. His face comes so close to my face that I hear his breath on my cheek.

My soul is possessed by the strength and glory of his Person. A desire arises within me to conquer and subdue him, to assert my independence of him and my lordship over him. I restrain myself, and become excited by the warm tenderness of his kind eyes.

Suddenly I embrace my Brother joyfully, intensely, passionately, and feel the same signs of his love towards me. I yield to the Christ, with no hatred or any doubt. The warmth of his brave body melts into my own warmth. I will never let my Saviour go.

6 October (Thursday)

I am thankful for a confident and peaceful spirit. I went, happier rather than fearful, to address grammar school boys on the purpose of education and the purpose of life. Perhaps now my education is beginning, and for that matter, my life.

7 October (Friday)

I went to testify to the goodness of one who had died, and noted in sadness the autumnal colours of the trees. But I rejoiced: the Friend is with me.

CHAPTER 13

JEALOUSY

8 October (Saturday)

It is apparent that Judas Iscariot a little before his betrayal gained for himself a prominent part in the Jesus movement. He was the treasurer and the secret and determined organizer. I believe that the evidence in the Gospels nearly compels us to conclude that his main purpose, as he aided the enemies of Jesus to capture him during the night and thus avoid commotion among the populace, was to hasten the saving suffering of the Anointed Son, thinking that the hosts of Heaven would come to save the Son of Promise and subjugate the kingdoms of the world and initiate the kingdom of the saints.

I wonder whether there was an element of jealousy and doubt in him? I think that every interpretation which maintains that jealousy and doubt were his main motives, a kind of poison lurking underneath the surface of his own Christian Piety, is mistaken. That is the tendency of Dorothy Sayers in that fickle drama series, *The Man Born to be King.*[1] A rash impatience rather than a savage cunning is suggested by the fragmentary history which is found in the Synoptic Gospels. But it is possible that there was a drop of poison in his heart as well, taking offence at the glory of Jesus as the Anointed One and as a Servant and to try and test him.

I know that there is some poison in me.

I cannot look at a painting of the Crucifixion without feeling that it was unfair to choose Jesus of Nazareth rather than the Brother of Low Degree to die for the sinners of the world.

9 October (The Lord's Day)

It is evident that one thing only is necessary for my healing. I must wrestle with my friend during the loneliness of the night.

I preached of his love, and knew in my own heart that the final battle between him and me would have to be fought before long.

I visited Powys and Adelheid and enjoyed their company immensely. Powys had been burning incense for fun and Rolff and Thydain put records on the gramophone – Euryl Coslett singing two noble tunes, 'Hyder' and 'Lausanne', and descending to a lower level to sing the incredible nonsense 'Once again my dear Wales'. Then we had the ballet music by Rosamunde Schubert, and everyone listened attentively to it and to Gounod's *Faust*.

*

After the boys had gone to bed Adleheid and Powys expressed amazement and even disgust that this Diary was so melancholic. I was surprised to hear such a complaint. I am not melancholy by nature, and I am certain that there is no hidden melancholy surfacing in these confessions. Acknowledging sin and looking the unpalatable truth in the face is enough to fill the most cheerful with grief, but even now, as I walk the *Via Purgativa*[2] – and I must, whatever others do, tread along this road as thoroughly as is possible – I receive comforting and happy experiences. I feel that I am leaping from depth to height and from height to depth and the two extremes progressively recede from one another. But I journey forward also and do not stand still, tossing and turning vainly and aimlessly. Or that is my hope, anyway.

10 October (Monday)

The colours of autumn change every hollow, hill and nook into a new pleasure to the eye and the imagination.

There is no sadness in the beauty of autumn. Dying to live, sinking to rise, being silent to sing again – all is part of the miracle for which none of us is sufficiently thankful.

11 October (Tuesday)

The ugliest of sins is jealousy. The sin is analysed as follows in *Yn y llyvyr hwnn: gogan* (which is abusing someone in his absence), *anghlod* (defaming another deceitfully in his absence), *absenair* (a noisy, backbiting defamation in another's absence), *clusthustingas* (hateful backbiting from an unworthy imagination to cause loss to another from animosity towards him), *dybrydrwydd* (the refusal to praise someone for his good deeds), *melltigo* (to throw suspicion on a good deed), *drygddychymyg* (accuse another of a new slander falsely), *digasedd* (brutalize a place or good fortune of another), *anghyweirdeb* (censure), *cas chwerwder, annundeb* (hating another, so that union with him is rejected), *gwatwar* (making fun to mock another), *cyhuddo, cas.*

I have already searched my soul with reference to some of these. Perhaps I should search further to get at those sneaky weeds, *dybydrwydd, melltigo* and *anghyweirdeb* – refusal to acknowledge good in others, doubting the motives of others in their beneficent deeds and being ungrateful, that is forgetting a kindness or being bilious towards a benefactor. Are these not the shoddiest things in life?

These things are closely related to the sin against the Holy Spirit. Here is Jesus going around doing good and his enemies asserting that he was healing not through the power of God but through the power of the Evil One – 'it is through the chief of the demons that he threw out demons'.[3] And the answer: 'How can Satan throw out Satan?' 'And so I tell you that people can be forgiven any sin and any evil they say, but whosoever says evil things against the Holy Spirit will not be forgiven, but he will be guilty of eternal judgement.' And the reason: 'Because they said that he had an evil spirit in him.'[4]

This is a warning, not a condemnation, a warning against condemnation. The ultimate condemnation will fall on the person who fails to see the goodness of goodness and the evil of evil. This is a far worse condition than the condition of the mad worshipper who bawls out 'Evil, be for me the Good.' The Sin against the Holy Spirit is the death of conscience and loyalty and mercy and of soul, the death of the self in the quicksand of self-worship and even hell is far too vain to swallow such endless corruption.

This is the void that God Himself cannot fill. This is the sin which rejects God and man and devil. This is the Non-existence which does not exist.

12 October (Wednesday)

The Way, the Truth and the Life, let me perceive and know and be; let me strive and arrive and be, now and for ever. Amen.

13 October (Thursday)

This is an opportunity to harvest with the saints once more, Calvinistic Methodist saints this time in one of the lovely valleys, lovely beyond words, which extend in the direction of the defiled crown of Mynydd Epynt. May the filth of Moloch be scrubbed off the fair face of Wales![5]

14 October (Friday)

Will Fuller came to see me unexpectedly, and his wife also, and this is the first time I have seen them since I returned from America in 1938. By now this half-Welsh exile is as American as any Canadian. But apart from this, he has not changed at all. And I, in the meantime, accepted the yoke of the Christ – and here I am still trying to learn to bear the yoke. 'Take my yoke upon you, and learn from me, because I am gentle and humble in spirit, and you will find rest. For the yoke I will give you is easy, and the load I will put on you is light.'[6]

15 October (Saturday)

Although jealousy is the most slimy of sins it is closely related to inducements which stimulated some of the greatest amongst the children of men: the desire to excel, the craving for fame and leadership, the sacred egoism.

It is very difficult for me to perceive my own sin in this.

I am a prophet. I pray that the world will accept the message which was given me: truth, peace, responsible freedom and sacrificial brotherhood, and the Saving Righteousness of the Living God who has glorified our lives with his Presence and Love and who calls on everyone to accept the ever-brilliant Privileges and the perfect Sonship in the Spirit. But my voice is one crying in the wilderness. The little congregation listens politely and tolerantly and tamely; and soon the dutiful worshippers turn towards their dinner or their supper, discussing the heat or the defect in the chapel, or the latest marvels in the world of sport or fashion or murder, or some local happening – frequently chatting kindly and warm-heartedly, but giving no attention to the sermon but, occasionally, turning to discuss, favourably or unfavourably, the voice or talent or the personality of the preacher.

Thousands and millions turn to the false prophets. Zion Chapel is overflowing with people who have come together to marvel at the well-known preacher from England who accepts the Scriptures literally and rejects their Spirit and scolds scurrilously crypto-pagans who wish to elevate the Spirit above the letter. And carriages and cars flock along road and rail conveying hundred of Welsh people to see the spiritual athletics at some arena in London and quake beneath the prophetic anger which avoids any mention of social wrongs and of warmongering politics – the kind of morality which considers an illegitimate child as more of a disgrace on humankind than the bomb which fell on Hiroshima.[7]

It is not jealousy but justice which is determined to speak out against the false and treacherous gospel which is able to compete with Elizabeth the Second and Dai Dower and Gilbert Harding for the publicity laurels in this dear land of Wales.[8]

16 October (The Lord's Day)

Here am I preaching Christ and him crucified – and everybody 'after supper' demanding to talk of Princess Margaret's courtship!

What is the religion of our country?

17 October (Monday)

It is not jealousy but justice which rejects the authority of publicity, the God of the Flies of the twentieth century. I know of fellow ministers who are poorer than me, of the occasional prophet, of the occasional reformer, of the occasional saint, who have been giving voice to the truth consistently and fairly from week to week for a few pounds and fewer thanks; and I heard some time ago of a certain superficial Welshman, who became famous in London as a slick broadcaster, receiving forty pounds in a coal-mining village in Wales for an empty lecture and even empty-headed admirers were disappointed.

It must be declared, for the sake of the mental health of society, that the standard of this age, its taste, its morality and its passion are low, and that the gods of the age are filth.

18 October (Tuesday)

From time to time the occasional prophet has dared to announce the Word of God in Vanity Fair. This was a fairly easy task when it was possible to locate the fair in a certain place and to know that it would be held at certain times of the year; but by today the fair is everywhere and its raucous noise is heard ceaselessly. The world now is an endless Vanity Fair; the new devices and the new methods of entertainment and amusement have guaranteed this.

A voice crying in the fair – not the wilderness – is the voice of truth now. Perhaps there is more hope for the stones of the wilderness than for the hearts of contemptible men of today.

I obtained gentle comfort from time to time in the great words which are found in Ezekiel: 'So tell them what I, the Sovereign Lord, am saying. I will gather them out of the countries where I scattered them, and will give the land of Israel back to them.

'When they return, they are to get rid of all the filthy, disgusting idols they find. I will give them a new heart and a new mind. I will take away their stubborn heart of stone and will give them an obedient heart. Then they will keep my laws and faithfully obey all my commandments. They will be my people and I will be their God.'[9]

But a heart of rock is a lot less intractable than a heart of dirt.

Oh Lord of Truth, Oh God of Eternal Goodness, Oh Holy Beauty
whom the flames of my soul can never reach, forgive me the rage
of fire which burns within me. For it is Your Own Fire. Otherwise,
destroy me, the Consuming Fire which will burn for ever.

19 October (Wednesday)

It was a kind of escape for me today to go and address a fellowship of women in a church in Monmouthshire. I told them about some of the women of the Gospels. The history of the Christian woman throughout the ages is extremely interesting. In the coalfield, very often, it is the wife who attends church while her husband attends the club.

20 October (Thursday)

I fear that I have not faced the accuser with reference to *dybrydrwydd* and *melltigo* and *anghyweirdeb*.

Draw near to me, the pale Stranger. I am beginning to love you.

'Refuse praise to another for his good deeds': I have heard others doing this many times, and often, to some extent, I have allowed the wrong. But I am a passive sinner rather than an active one, in this matter. So again with regard to 'showering suspicion on a good deed'. I have often seen unworthy motives ascribed, without foundation, to benefactors, and my sin, sometimes, is in listening to an ungracious innuendo without opposing it or denying it. But I do not find any pleasure in mistrust without cause: that is too much like spending a great deal of money on an inappropriate book.

Are you guilty of ingratitude? I don't believe that I am guilty of the more crude forms. I do not detest a benefactor. I do not deliberately try to untie the bonds of friendship and mutual understanding. But it is so easy to forget. I know that friends have come and gone. I well remember some who have enriched my life with their love and laughter and sorrows and hopes but who are by now so far from me as the Southern Cross.

I call their names to mind.

Oh Father, may your mercy embrace all my friends and lovers. Perfect the affections of the past in the Love which was and is and will be to eternity.

21 October (Friday)

Thanks for good company and for a good cause!

22 October (Saturday)

When I marvel at any masterpiece of the right kind – poem, painting, novel, oratorio, building, sculpture, essay, witticism, sonata, sermon, epigram, folk tale, reasoning, description, drama – I experience, within the limits of my taste, great joy and delight; not the drunken, excited-until-I-lose-my-senses joyousness which I experienced as a youth but a kind of spiritual elevation and release whose nature I do not fully understand. But often, painfully often, jealousy lurks in the depths of the experience – the jealousy of Cain. I am jealous when I admire someone. The greater the admiration the deeper the jealousy. I am not referring to the fact that I am more critical than in the past: healthy admiration is not possible without criticism. But egoism too often sours and at the same time sharpens my appreciation. This is not true of my appreciation of an art form that I have no interest in pursuing myself: architecture for example. And strangely enough neither is it true of the joy I experience on hearing an honest sermon. I admire preaching without being jealous. One of the privileges of my life is to worship under the ministry of students on Saturday morning, and it is a pleasure to see the variety of the gifts of the Holy Spirit.[10]

*

I went to address a political meeting tonight and dashed into the town where I am to minister tomorrow. The pillar saints[11] would have considered my life to be extremely worldly.

23 October (The Lord's Day)
Sometimes I preach more pugnaciously than usual. There is a noisy battle being fought between the heights and depths of the universe, and there are drops of blood on the Milky Way. Every sermon should be part of that battle.

The battle is in my heart as well.

The duality between good and evil can not be avoided, and should not be attempted. Perhaps it is a duality within the unity of the universe, and that Satan must, as in the Book of Job, provide God with a fairly fulsome report of his various activities. But the old Captain has sufficient resources for that activity: resources and verses.

24 October (Monday)
Recently someone congratulated me on being elected the President of the World and asked whether the Pope had sent me a note wishing me well in my stewardship. A small piece in the press by a mischievous rascal is responsible for this: that is the prize, or the cost, of taking on the chairmanship

of some committee which is unlikely to meet but once in a
while.

I always despised publicity. I remember the difficulty the
editor of a local newspaper had in eliciting from me details of
some minor success which came to me unexpectedly when I
was a schoolboy.

I have been guilty many times of dreaming of some kind
of fame – fame without seeking it, something totally different
from repugnant publicity. I did not seek to see my name in
large letters in the newspaper or to hear it on the lips of
the *profanum vulgas*.[12] Rather, I longed for friendship with
Zarathustra and Laotze, Euripides and Catallus, Jeremiah
and Origen, Dante and Dafydd ap Gwilym, Michelangelo
and Morgan Llwyd, Pantycelyn and Beethoven, Dostoevsky
and Tagore.[13] I longed for the friendship of Williams Parry,
although I have never ventured to visit him nor have I met
him at all. Apparently Yeats desired to have a meal, at the end
of the journey, with Landor and Donne. By now, the longing
has become part of a more passionate desire in my experience
– the desire to sit with Abraham and Isaac and Jacob in the
Kingdom of God.

And yet I know I am jealous of all of them. I am jealous of
God!

25 October (Tuesday)

*Christ Jesus, visit your yearning friend. Come to me, with your
gentle laugh and merciful touch. Come to eat and chat and sleep in
my home. Gladden my life with your holy graces. Embrace me with
your gentle truth. Dignify my flesh with your kiss of peace. I have no
brother but You – You and your brothers! Come to me, come to me.*

And he came – for one ecstatic moment – the brown eyes, the
scar, the smile, the warmth of the blood on the skin of his face
and the unbearable, heroic, brilliant love.

26 October (Wednesday)

The Tarrell valley is a miracle of autumnal beauty: an eloquent witness to the hidden fire which is burning beneath our feet.[14]

27 October (Thursday)

I am not envious of unworthy fame. That is not worth having. I do not understand how the occasional artist has gone to a great deal of trouble to acquire a name for himself by misappropriating the work of another artist. I do not understand how an author can seek fame among his contemporaries by following some unsubstantial fashion. Fame without merit is vanity. Any prize that is not given by God is a shameful debt. The approbation of the world, the approval of the masses, the honours of the idolatrous rabble – all these things are as glorious as a fortune that has been won on the football pools.

'I assure you, they have already been paid in full.'[15] There is no more damning verdict.

Because they are deserving, because they are worthy, and not because of their prizes, am I envious of the great ones whose greatness is acknowledged by my soul.

It is not the fame but the achievement which makes one long to be like them: yes, even the achievement of the Cross.

'The attitude you should have is the attitude that Christ Jesus had: He always had the nature of God, but he did not think that by force he should try to remain equal to God. Instead of this, of his own free will he gave up all he had, and took the nature of a servant. He became like a human being and appeared in human likeness. He was humble and walked the path of obedience all the way to death – his death on the cross. For this reason God raised him to the highest place above and gave him the name that is greater than any name. And so, in honour of the name of Jesus all beings in heaven, on earth, and in the world below will fall on their knees, and all will openly proclaim that Jesus Christ is Lord, for the glory of God the Father.'[16]

I find my heaven and hell in these incomparable words:

The distance between them was vast
He filled it with his own merit.[17]

28 October (Friday)

I was able to eat tonight not with Abraham and Isaac and Jacob, and not with Deutro-Isaiah or Pseudo-Dionysius either, but with some of the knights-in-waiting of our public life in Wales and two knights already ordained. Also, the account would be an interesting appendix to *Ym Mêr Fy Esgyrn* by Mr T I Ellis.[18]

Oh that I could but peal the bell and see Arthur rising!

29 October (Saturday)

I said goodbye to a committee or council which I have served for more than six years. I had a great deal of pleasure in its conferences and I learnt a lot. It was an opportunity also to form alliances for the occasional good cause. There is a hint of wistfulness on closing the book after reaching the end of an interesting chapter.

As I travelled home I saw Castell Coch near Tongwynlais enchantingly noble against the colours of autumn. The whole scene looked crudely 'romantic' but I was not in a critical temper. The rest of the journey was happy. This is the happiness that comes on reading a poem which refuses to let go of the heart. A thrush sang within me.

30 October (The Lord's Day)

It was a pleasure after my travels to be able to preach in the locality and sleep at home last night and tonight.

*

We discussed the fortunes of a friend of ours after the service, myself and a few companions. He is one who is always unhappy about his lot, one who is always seeking something better and who believes that a better country is a certain reward for the one who is willing to change direction. 'The grass is greener...,' one of us said.

There is nothing that is more typically Welsh than 'The grass is greener...' Longing: 'I hope for what is to come'; the magic isle, the land of fairies, the Lowland Hundred. Avallon: 'my love lives over the sea', 'way over the wave', the Canaan above, my Father's house, the pomegranates of the land, the hills of Jerusalem; the perigrini, Bardsey Island, predictive utterances, the crown of the island, the crowns of heaven, another elevation for a Welshman, becoming a salmon or an eagle, 'a brighter horizon', to swallow Gwion Bach and to give birth to Taliesin.[19] And I, safe out of their reach, 'Swimming in love and peace.'[20]

The longing for escape, the longing of the slave, as we see in the spiritual songs of the American Negro: how can we escape this?

31 October (Monday)

Once, when I had just started preaching, I frightened the occasional Nonconformist by including in my public prayers a translation of the *Anima Christi*:[21]

> Anima Christi, sanctifica me.
> Corpus Christi, salva me.
> Sanguis Christi, inebria me.
> Aqua lateris Christi, lava me.
> Splendor vultus Christi, illumina me.

This prayer was of great assistance to me to enliven my love of Christ at that time. Under the influence of a Christian kind of devotion – and there is plenty in the Welsh hymns – the imprecise *élan vital* became a Living Person. I came to know Christ as a Companion and Friend. My love was revived many times on meditating on old Latin hymns.

Jesu, dulcis memoria,
Dans vera cordis gaudia;
Sed super, mel et omnia
Eius dulcis praesentia.

Jesu, dulcedo cordium,
Fons vivus, lumen mentium,
Excedens omne gaudium
Et omne desiderium.

Salutis humanae Sator,
Jesu voluptas cordium,
Orbis redempti Conditor,
Et casta lux amantium.

Amor Jesu dulcissime,
Quando cor nostrum visitas,
Pellis mentis caliginem,
Et nos reples dulcedine.

Iesu, Rex admirabilis
Et Triumphator nobilis,
Dulcedo ineffeabilis,
Totus desirabilis.[22]

I remember when I was a theological student, shocking my landlady, who was a submissive Anglo-Catholic, by singing 'O quanta qualia'[23] when having a bath.

On second thoughts, it is part of the work of the Holy Spirit on earth and in purgatory to reconcile Peter Abelard and Bernard of Clairvaux.

CHAPTER 14

PRIDE

1 November (Tuesday)

Like every preacher I must lower my head under the occasional flood of flattery. 'Simple', 'unassuming', 'humble' – but I know that my greatest sin is pride, hidden sin, sin of the soul – not the superficial vanity or self-confidence, not the pride in talent or intelligence, but that pride which demands that the universe be a stage for the amazing drama of the pompous ego.

With such pride possessing my heart I can afford to be patient and humble and comparatively fair to everybody.

2 November (Wednesday)

I might as well look at Pride or Arrogance as it is analysed in *Yn y Llyvyr hwn: ymfychaw* (skulking), *bocsachu* (boasting), *ymdrychafael* (abuse), *annostwng* (insolence), *drudannaeth* (cruelty), *ymchwyddaw* (to be puffed up), *cynhennu* (quarrelling), *annoddef* (intolerance), *anufudd-dawd* (obstinacy), *tremyg* (contempt), *rhag ymgymryd* (presumption), *cellwair* (mockery), *geu-grefydd* (heresy), *trallafariaeth* (loud-mothed), *tra achub* (seizing too much), *clod orwag* (empty praise).[1]

Of these, insolence, being puffed up, obstinacy and presumption are closely related – refusing to respect 'superiors' or the 'aged'. I believe that some respect is due to the elderly since they have lived longer than the young; the abundance of days demands some honour and some special gentleness. But I do not believe in Methuselah as the Saviour of the World.

There is too much *amor temporis acti* in the minds of the old for us to trust their wisdom completely. It is stupid to put the government in the hands of the elderly and force the young to fight wars. If the order was otherwise there would be better hope for us to put an end to wars soon. As for the 'superiors', talent, genius, conviction and culture and true nobility should be respected, but there are very many acknowledged 'superiors' of our society that do not deserve but the smallest grain of respect on account of these things. Inheritance should also be respected, certainly – as long as we remember that a country's inheritance is far more important than the inheritance of a lord, that the labourer's scar is more glorious than the scar of a soldier and that the succession of the saints is much more apostolic than the succession of bishops.

It is so easy, when I discuss my own sin, to turn and discuss the sins of the age and the sins of the world.

I must face the others on the list.

3 November (Thursday)

Quarrelling and intolerance are more closely related to hatred than pride.

I must plead guilty to a good number of the others: *ymfychaw* (which is finding it difficult to endure anyone 'of equal status and rank'); *bocsachu* (which is 'a man taking what is not his'); *ymddyrchafael* ('to excel whilst being contemptuous of others'); *cellwair* ('unruly abuse by playful mockery'); *tra achub* ('a desire to gain honour for the sake of transitory fame'); *clod orwag* ('failing to give praise to God for deeds'). I am also guilty of *drudaniaeth*, which is 'dwelling mentally on evil', stubbornness in wickedness. On the other hand, I do not feel that I sin through *drallafariaeth* (unless this diary is an example of the sin), which is 'to release too much empty speech'; nor through *tremyg* either except to the degree that *tremyg* is contained within *ymddyrchafael*.

It is probable that *geu grefydd* ('to hide faults and to show achievements that were not there') is synonymous with hypocrisy.[2] One of the aims of this diary is to drive all hypocrisy out of my life. But hypocrisy can play tricks even with open confession.

4 November (Friday)

Jesus Christ, the good Doctor, give me your health. Pour the oil of your mercy and the wine of your sacrifice in my wounds. Make me a new man in you.

*

Despite his face on a Friday
Despite his great pain on a stake.[3]

5 November (Saturday)

Rhiwallon has been away and McTavish forgot Guy Fawkes. I'll have to Cymricize this festival: the Festival of the Red Dragon, perhaps. In its present form there is no appeal in the nonsense, and no purpose except noise and flash. Perhaps the fireworks are a symbol to some people, a symbol of destroying the enemy; and the enemy, according to the hidden compulsions of those involved in the fun, is the Government or Guy Fawkes – the *status quo* or the opponents of the *status quo*. But symbolising the fun is more purposeful than this. The Welsh-language and Welsh societies ought to possess it and make it a symbol of the fire of the Dragon which wills the overthrow of the castles of oppression and injustice and hate.

However, we had a quiet night. May God reconcile between Guy Fawkes and King James.

6 November (The Lord's Day)

By now the valley of the Tarrell appears as if it has burnt out. Embers and coals are everywhere, but what beauty. And it is full of promise and comfort and testimony.

'The summer always dies to live.'[4] Through it all life flows, and the Lord sits on the flood.

During the afternoon I went to worship with the Baptists and relished the sermon keenly. It is a pleasure to see a man's character and heart verifying his message. And even better was it to hear the minister who presided praying on God to give us 'the Living Thing'.

Thing or Person? But the living Thing, anyway; and the Person who is greater than anyone or anything living in it.

*

When I preached in the evening I spoke of the difference between Creator and Creation.

I am a creature. That is a truth I have difficulty in understanding and accepting.

I can live with the uncomfortable fact that I am a sinner. This can be interpreted in a fairly consoling way and the claim made that I have not finished growing, I have not reached the goal – although the Accuser is whispering this minute that my history, perhaps, is to wither and not to grow, and that I am not, in my inmost soul, even running towards the goal. But if I can admit fairly freely that I am a sinner there is something in my soul which is unwilling to admit that I am a creature – that I have no right to live except the right given me by God.

Am I a child of Time, without any knowledge of Eternity? Is Nothingness the Mystery from whose bowels my life flew and is Nothingness the Mystery which, after I have been a little contemptuous *(ymdrychafael),* and boasted *(bocsachu)* and skulked *(ymfachaw),* will swallow my life for ever? The flower of the field, the insect of the mire, the seed of spermatozoa in the sap of secret places – and all our history is the same, some excitement between silence and silence?

What is a Creature?

What is a Creator?

'The sun rises with its blazing heat and burns the plant; its flower falls off, and its beauty is destroyed.'[5]

Is that all?

But I had better finish. This diary is becoming too much like a long poem from the last century, a list of questions in the manner of the New Poet which has now become so old. Fading, falling, losing – that is also the history of poetry.

7 November (Monday)

I had tea in a palace, and the welcome was princely. I never expected to go to such a place or to experience such fellowship.

*

Let Plutus speak. Pluto has the last word.[6]

> I saw one shaking under the oppression of the Arch torturer.
> My heart melted in pity.

*

Tragedy and comedy are twins.

Who was the first person who saw the devil in the painting *Salem*? The Evil One is comical and cunning.[7] But God is the Supreme Laugher, First and Last.

8 November (Tuesday)

A great experience today was to hear an extremely powerful address on the meaning of Sunday for Christians. I did not think that anyone could preach on the subject – that is, present the majesty of the Gospel and its challenge to our age, and the Judgement and Grace of the Almighty.

Without fellowship in Christ, a worshipful, committed fellowship, the observance of a day is only a false convention. It is only one answer which the Church has for the world, that is her life; and the life of the Church is the Kingdom: Gospel and Health and Sacrifice, the Maker and Operator and Comforter.

*

199

I heard of troubles after returning home, 'Whatever happens or can happen has already happened before', as the poet said.[8]

9 November (Wednesday)

I made another journey to Monmouthshire and led the worship at a church which had been loyal to the Welsh language but which is flagging under the pressure. My topic was the Church, and the pride which soils wealth and success.

The Welsh word *syberwyd* is a strange word. We did our best to put a shine on the word 'superbia'. The English word 'superb' is an example of the same effort. It is possible to be 'proud' and *syber* in a good sense and in a bad sense.

10 November (Thursday)

I took services in the same place – in Welsh in the afternoon and in English in the evening. Worship and sacrifice, dedication and love, knowing ourselves as the means and God as the Mediator – there is no other way of deliverance.

*

Oh God my Father, let me know myself by knowing You.

11 November (Friday)

Wales and Eternity were the major topics for Ben Bowen, and I heard that Eternity was the only topic for Moelwyn.[9]

Has the word got terror or comfort for me? I recall some of the German hymns on the subject:

O Ewigkeit, du Donnerwort,
O Schwert, das durch die Seele bohhrt.

and,

O Ewigkeit, du Freudenwort,
Das mich erquikket fort und fort.[10]

And the old, strange hymn 'O Ewigkeit, O Ewigkeit' which talks of the perfect circle, and the eternal Now at its centre – and the Choice and the Judgement.

How does one face Eternity? As Lord or as Servant?

Behold Jesus in his gentleness coming to me. He can overburden me without annihilating me, overcome me without killing me, possess me without degrading me.

12 November (Saturday)

At times of good weather there are some who are ready to say that we must pay for the beauty by suffering bad weather later on. I know of one man who always says, on every fine day in the summer, 'We'll have to pay for this later on.' The sentence is a simple and comprehensive expression of one philosophy of life.

There is an element of truth in the philosophy. Everything must be paid for, somehow, some time. Nevertheless, it is an incomplete and insufficient philosophy. I prefer the other side of the coin, the carpe diem,[11] 'Sufficient for me the beauty of the moment.'

The present moment is quite fair. Today I arrived at my birthday once again, and the love of my dear ones drowns every feeling of 'time flies' snitching the years of my life from me. Anna and Taranwen confirm the claim made in Culhwch ac Olwen[12] that women are God's gift – a claim that summarises Wales's message for Europe. I rejoice in the children as well, the keenness and correctness of McTavish, the musing and love of Flanagan, the innocence and sympathy of Ap Siencyn – and their affable friend, Rhiwallon, and gentle Arfon, next door. It pleases my spirit also to think of my neighbours and fellow workers and friends, and the warmth that lies between me and the lively young souls that have been entrusted to my care.

I remember the promise to Jesus' disciples: 'houses and brothers and sisters and mothers and children and lands, together with persecutions; and in the world to come, eternal life.'[13]

Yes, it is joy to be allowed to live. And yet I have reason to believe that stormy clouds are gathering on the horizon of my life. I am enjoying life – but I will have to pay for this later on.

13 November (The Lord's Day)

The Providence of God, the responsibility of man, the spiritual Reality – it is a great privilege to be able to preach these.

Another privilege today was enjoying a conversation with a Christian scholar, a diligent worker and notable stylist, and I had an opportunity to appreciate his orderly and concise mind. I felt, as I listened to him, that he was a complete man, and I am so incomplete, full of cravings and yearnings and unfulfilled possibilities.

I know, of course, that I am still reluctant to consider my own sins.

14 November (Monday)

I visited the art exhibition held by the Swansea Art Society. And I was disappointed. The noteworthy artist in it is Colin Jones. He has a future, I hope. 'Symbol', 'atmosphere', 'expression' – that is the only way for the arts now. There must be a marriage of Caer Pedryfan and Byzantium.[14]

In the evening I went to a meeting of Christians and non-Christians to discuss the challenge of nuclear warfare which is threatening the nations. A few of us were representing Christian pacifism and others at the other extreme who believed that war and even the hydrogen bomb could be a godly weapon. There was important support for the idea that war can sometimes be just but that it cannot be just in the new situation which has been caused by the loathsome atomic bomb. I have nothing but contempt for two arguments that were put forward tonight: the argument that the hydrogen bomb had to be made to delay the outbreak of the next war and thus guarantee a period of peace; and the argument that the important thing is not the bomb, but sin, and therefore we must 'face sin' rather than throwing our weight behind a movement to eradicate the bomb or to abolish war. The last argument was presented in the manner of the traditional theology and also (and the word 'tension' being used instead of the word 'sin'!) in the manner of secular humanism; and the two methods are totally fallacious.

I used to be fed up with theologizing about sin in order to avoid talking about the sins which are painful for men to think about. I heard a preacher say that 'Sin with a capital S' is the only human problem that should be considered – and the conclusion was that the preacher should not bother to touch the conscience of his congregation by talking about sins like theft and murder. What would Amos have to say about this profound doctrine?

15 November (Tuesday)

I have not spoken much about my work in this diary. It is impossible to provide public details of the joys and tribulations of this particular ministry which has been entrusted to me, and to that extent these personal records have had to be one-sided and misleading. For my work is an important part of my life, and many of my 'spiritual' experiences have been joined with the lives which touch my life as a result of the responsibility put upon me.

Today I have been forced to look with astonishment at the possibility that my work could fail, and fail catastrophically.[15]

I think of my work mainly as a pastor in a community of Christians who are preparing to lead their fellow Christians in the general ministry. My work is part of the ministry, and the community here is a kind of church – an intermittent church which has been called together for a particular purpose. I am a minister, a servant: not a master. I am a 'minister' not a 'magister'. This means that I serve a brotherhood, and that our common life ought to be different from the kind of community that is found in secular colleges.

Little by little, I have been encouraging the brothers along this road, without bickering and partisanship. It is clear to me that some are unable to see my methods or my aims, but my feeling, even today, is that we are moving in the right direction.

But today we have an explosion, and the whole carriage is shaking throughout.

16 November (Wednesday)

It is *Dies Irae* everywhere. There is no escaping the lancets.

> *Oh gentle Lord, be merciful to us. You are the Minister from Whom all the ministry in heaven and on earth is named. Minister to us in this affliction. Amen.*

There is a glimmer of hope.

17 November (Thursday)

I am able to breathe freely once more, and Thalia tries to tickle Melpomene.[16]

*

A man has plenty of opportunity to study pride by observing his contemporaries. But my subject is my own iniquity. I see that criticism does not lessen my pride nor does it shake my egoism. There is something about me which makes me laugh at my critics. It is I who am right, even in spite of my own failures. I am prepared to confess these, but the ego boasts even in the mud and muck.

18 November (Friday)

I am too tired today to record anything, but it is obvious that there are new battles to be fought before long.

19 November (Saturday)

Recent days have been a little tiresome, but I am certain today that integrity will arise out of the turmoil. The river is flowing more rapidly than I wished, but its flow is in the right direction.

*

I recall my interest in the subject of self-government in education, namely the self-government of pupils in the educational community, the school or the college. I have always been convinced that there is no value in imposing discipline on children from the outside only – or on young people or adults either. The only true discipline – as has been claimed by educationists who are unwilling to take a gamble on their own theories – is self-discipline. In any community this means collective discipline, living together and sharing responsibility and interest and culture. This is the true education, and the reason that it is not found in our schools is that the majority of parents and teachers believe that the purpose of education is to instruct children in the art of gaining wealth and position in the world. Success is their aim, the kind of success that is signified by a certificate and a favourable bank statement.

*

A Christian academy gives the opportunity to seek the true education and the true discipline and the true community.

20 November (The Lord's Day)
I am too proud to despair.

*

I enjoyed myself last night and today in the company of a studious man whom I once knew, an enthusiastic savourer of English literature and a friend of John Cowper Powys and Huw Menai,[17] one who is disposed to admire the eminences of the literary journals and television. I am sometimes tempted to claim that Powys is the only well-known Anglo-Welshman who deserves a second reading, but my host is kinder towards his contemporaries.

*

Time, Death, Immortality, Resurrection: a kind of spiritual giddiness came over me when I had a glimpse of these imponderables as I preached today. I felt like someone who could see the depths from the top of a steep, high, turreted crag and I failed to hold on.

I am jealous of the Eternal, and I crawl in the corruption of History.

21 November (Monday)

There is something which compels me to examine my pride, although my soul fights fiercely against such torment.

My worst sin is feeling that I Myself am the centre of the universe. My greatest need is some kind of Copernican revolution in my heart, some proof that I rotate around God and not God rotating around me.

How common is this sin?

Despite my critical nature there are some people I can admire ungrudgingly. When I am convinced of someone's gift or genius, of the value of a poem, of the brilliance of a speech, I am able to praise fervently and sincerely. I am willing to acknowledge merit in others. But as I acknowledge, as I utter the warmest words, I can hear someone whispering in my ear that I am the King and that a word of praise from my lips is more precious that the loud acclamations of the world.

That is my fundamental transgression. I knew this from the beginning in my heart. That is why I chose the nom-de-plume 'The Brother of Low Degree'. The name wounds me – not because it places me low on the list but because it makes me one among my brothers.

I am willing to be generous, gentle, laudable, humble, willing to serve, on one condition – that the archangels crown me the highest.

I reject the Sacrifice of the Predestined. 'He gave up all he had, and took the nature of a servant. He became like a human being.'[18]

This terrifies me. Am I not the Higher Man?

Ymfychaw: a failure to see anyone 'high or equal'; refusing to give up all; refusing to devalue oneself; refusing to be incarnate.

I know that there is no one else in the world who is willing to acknowledge my higher manhood. I also know that the Almighty in the mystery of his Providence is teaching me that I am one among many. Was not Taranwen sent to teach me that the Brother of Low Degree is an accurate description of me? Was I not dragged into the ministry, work which is despised so much by the best people? Have I not been forced to kneel before some who are slaves by nature but who have been elevated to princes among the people? Have I not been prevented by a thousand hindrances from fulfilling the feats which I was ordered to accomplish? I. Prometheus, Melchisedec, Krishna, Lleu,[19] Son of Man.

22 November (Tuesday)

Am I not a boaster, the most impudent *poseur* since the Serpent of Eden? Has there ever been a cry *de profundis* more mischievous than this diary? Does not this blight of self-aggrandizement corrupt every letter?

And yet I give a thorough scouring to my wriggling and screeching soul. The Brother of Low Degree will probably surface from the water naked and clean.

23 November (Wednesday)

I remember the cold words uttered by my friend Gerallt to me about the diary. 'From the depths of my despair I call to you!' he said ironically, and his scorn was like a cold shower on my back.

24 November (Thursday)

My Mother, my Mother, I have always wondered at your cleanliness. I know that You are busy collecting the dust of the universe, and

scrubbing the floors of the world. I know too that you wash Your
children's clothes and iron them skilfully for Sunday. Thank You for
the water of Your mercy and the soap of Your truth on my quaking
soul. Wash me and I shall be as white as snow.
  Come to me my Mother. I want to see Your beloved face.

25 November (Friday)

I remember that I greatly relished a popular little song by
O Madog Williams in the dialect of industrial east Glamorgan,
a song which describes 'Shân' the mother washing the body
of her boy in a tub, scrubbing the little one with painful
thoroughness so that he would be clean and attractive:

> A moment like this is a part of heaven,
> And Shân is so much like God:
> If she is poor, she's only got to look at Will,
> And she is overjoyed.

> I just imagine that God
> Thinks the world of Shân
> 'Cos she goes to so much trouble in such a filthy place
> To keep the little one so clean.

It is not without purpose that in Welsh the Spirit of God is
called the 'Clean Spirit'.

CHAPTER 15

THE DIVIDE

26 November (Saturday)

I must record an exciting and terrible dream: a loathsome monster mocking me and grasping me and I, as I defended myself, beat him wildly. I woke in grief.

*

I was troubled by fatigue all day until I started on my journey with Rhiwallon. We had tea with his uncle and aunt, and the conversation was charming and free. I then went to the meeting house and met old friends, old students of the college, and received a fulsome welcome in the home of kind friends. It is surprising how the spirit opens in fellowship as a flower opens in the sunshine.

*

But in the silence of the night, my grief returns to me. The monster: what is it but the Spirit which exalted itself against the self-denying Love? The Unclean Spirit, the Lord of the Abyss, the King of the Dirt.

27 November (The Lord's Day)

Warm the welcome, kind the listening, pleasant the fellowship – but I know that the longing which draws me to Christ also keeps me far from him.

I am going to be like God. I know that God's voice

encourages me to be like him, but sometimes a voice scorches my soul and says that I am a God, Creator and Sustainer and Saviour, and that the whole world would disappear if I refused to vindicate him.

'You will be like God and know what is good and bad.'[1]

'You must be perfect as your Father in heaven is perfect',[2] the Preacher of the Mountain said.

The gulf between these two admonitions is the split in my heart.

28 November (Monday)

I had some conversation with Eiddig Pugh recently, a brother to Cardod. This is an example of pride becoming vanity and impotence and confusion. Poor fellow, and his attempt to appear witty and clever, perceptive and mature, highbrow and haughty: all the artifice was so weak and false.

His bile is choking him.

29 November (Tuesday)

I long once more for fellowship with Christ, for the blessing of his touch, for the consolation of his voice, for the gentle strength of his smile. There is some river flowing between us, some gap separating us, some frightening rift impedes the old affection.

My imagination is too weak to discern him in the gentleness and majesty of his flesh.

Oh that I could see him like Thomas in the past! Oh that I could be but amazed by him and whisper 'My Lord and my God'![3] Oh could I but know and love him, the scarred Christ, the suffering God-man!

My Father who are in heaven and in the slime of the earth also,
Who dwells in the Light that cannot be approached and Who
works in the light which blesses every insect and eagle and wolf
and man, Who addressed the formless void and the heart of Your
servant, Who drew form from purpose, and life from form, and

love from life, and glory from love, You the Unchanging Flood, the
Living Being, hear me. I am yours. Heal the flow of blood from
my soul, make whole the rent in my heart. Give me Your Peace,
give me Your Christ, give me Your Noonday. Drown every untruth
in the Truth as it is Christ Jesus. Eradicate all self-worship in the
Friendship which knows no boundary or ebb. For His Name's sake.
Amen.

30 November (Wednesday)

I have tried to know Jesus once more by means of the sensuous imagination.

I tried to force myself to stand by his side. I tried to roll the centuries and miles together and to destroy the chains of time and distance. And although the flesh was willing, the spirit was weak. I struggled, I pressed, I worried, until my soul was harassed.

And a morose trance came over me, a sluggishness, a spiritual torpor. And I slipped and sank and fell until I felt my feet on the inhospitable ground of the wilderness. The aridity and hot wind were all-consuming, and Satan's deadly domain extended without pity on every hand.

I eventually saw him, the Christ, Jesus, Son of the Carpenter, Son of Man. He was standing pensively beside a large stone. The divine anger and the eternal gentleness shone in his eyes.

I heard a fervent voice saying 'Follow me'. But it was not the voice of Jesus. It was I who had called, and I hated my own voice.

*

Here we are ascending and the whole world is giddily wild, until I reach the top of the mountain. I looked, and saw with remarkable clarity: colours and forms and curves, livelier and sharper than anything I had previously experienced: houses and cities and civilizations dancing around me, magic and fantasy, fleeting glories that have been and will be, fair towers, flying chariots, scarlet and golden mantles.

Jesus looked on silently, and his eyes were pronouncing mercy.

I heard my own voice once more, although the noise of the wind and the bustle of the world were screaming in my ears. My voice rose to a lightening-like screech which darted hither and thither as if it was trying to escape from the chamber of creation. And this is what the voice said: 'All this I will give you, if you fall down and worship me.'

I saw the miraculous smile of Jesus and I heard his reply like a whisper in my heart: 'Away with you, Satan; for it is written, "Worship the Lord your God and serve only him."'[4]

*

I know myself. I hate myself.

1 December (Thursday)

Here I return from the 'inner life' to the 'outward life' with a leap through the void.

This is an important day. Fly the flags.

The Way and the Truth and the Life! Even in the life of a college one must choose and know and live.

2 December (Friday)

Yesterday is like dream, and it is as distant and as exciting as the battle of Thermopylae.[5] I hear the blows and screams; I am amazed at the contesting and strutting; I appreciate the desire for glorifying goodness and for verifying a principle.

And within me there is another battle. Who has a claim on me? Is it the Eternal or Myself?

I lost him once again, the Broken One who Makes Whole.

It is incredible that the sun rises and sets and the wheel of time turns.

3 December (Saturday)

I lost the young Nazarene, brave of heart and strong to heal.

But a Presence surrounds me: the Accuser is closing in on me.

I feel very lonely today, wretchedly separated from my fellow men. I am a shaking potentate on my golden throne, and my defenders lying in their blood on the floor of the hall, and my enemies stretching their arms to grasp me.

And yet I have only one Enemy, and he fills my world.

*

The train journey was comfortable and the welcome was warm. It was easy to open my heart to friends and to go to bed late but more satisfied as a result.

But one burnt offering is ready, and no one except God can sacrifice it, and no one can sacrifice it but me.

CHAPTER 16

RATS

4 December (The Lord's Day)

The bridegroom, the Anointed One, the Dazzling White, Happy and Gentle Resurrected One is the paramount Object of my three sermons today.

I know that I love Him and that I desire to love Him more. I have a passionate longing to embrace and cherish Him. The psychoanalysts are welcome to interpret the longing in their own way: sex, ambition, a complex. I only know that I have this insatiable desire.

*

There is the Criminal on His Cross. I see Him clearly from a distance, a sack of red flesh, projecting pitifully into sight in the light of the soldiers' torches in the vast darkness of the world. I approach Him. I run. I fly. I rush upon Him.

*

It is not the Christ who is before me, but the Magna Mater, the all-embracing Carnality, the Harlot with multiple teats, whose resources are bountiful. My life is a willing and eager sacrifice on her fiery altar.[1]

*

Very often this is the theme in paintings of Saint Anthony's temptation: the Crucified One changing into an enchanting prostitute. I also remember an experience I had as a youth, seeing the Object on the Cross as a mother to all the nations and writing a sonnet to express the wonder. The sonnet was published in my college magazine. I recall that I described the nations growing like a mouse in the womb.

*

Losing the Christ: that is my story once more.

5 December (Monday)

I departed amicably from friends and turned homewards.

My friend Powys mentioned more than once about the strange prominence which is given to the mouse in some of the things that I have written.

According to Aristotle, in every tragedy there is pity and terror. Sometimes I pitied the little mouse and laughed on seeing the terror of the woman in its presence; I was fearful when I caught a glimpse of a rat hiding in its uncomfortable hole in a wall near my home and I felt agonies of pity in the face of the uncompromising enmity towards it on the part of men.

In the ancient world the snake was man's natural enemy; today the enemy which is most hated is the rat.

The lovely grey squirrel has been damned in our day by giving it a bad reputation, that is 'the tree rat'. And although the grey squirrel is a hideous sinner (especially in the eyes of the pretty darling, the red squirrel) one could not find a better example of unprincipled propaganda in our time than this savage nickname.

D H Lawrence respects the snake as one of the gods of life, but the rat is no more than the incarnation of evil for him.

What strange grace prompts me to address the rat as a particular comrade in the chaos of the cosmos?

6 December (Tuesday)

Greetings, friend; greetings, king of the sewers.

7 December (Wednesday)

A host of thoughts about the last days of Jesus' earthly life came to my mind. I see him standing in the temple precincts and on the streets, and I know that it is I who am examining and cross-examining him – concerning a tribute to Caesar, the fate of mankind, the ancestry of the Anointed One, yes, and about the most important commands of the law. I see Jesus proffering the bread and the wine, and I know that I am dipping with him in the dish. I hear his voice talking of the coming of the Son of Man on the clouds of heaven, and I know that I want to spit on him and cover his face and slap him and say 'Prophesy'. I hear the frightful, heart-breaking cry and I mock: 'He saved others but he cannot save himself.'[2]

8 December (Thursday)

'Let us see the Messiah, the King of Israel, come down from his cross now, and we will believe in him.'[3] And again: 'He was humble and walked the path of obedience all the way to death – his death on the cross. For this reason God raised him to the highest place above and gave him the name that is greater than any other name. And so, in honour of the name of Jesus all beings in heaven, on earth, and in the world below will fall on their knees, and all will openly proclaim that Jesus Christ is Lord, to the glory of God the Father.'[4]

> *Oh Lord Jesus, affront me with your forgiveness, shame me with your love, be a Brother for ever to the Brother of Low Degree. For the sake of that Name. Amen.*

9 December (Friday)

I travelled the *Via Purgativa* and I feel that I am coming to the end of that journey. I do not know whether there will be other journeys after this – the *Via Illuminativa* and the *Via Unitiva* which the mystics spoke about. I will not ask.[5]

Here I am like a pilgrim approaching the cell of the hermit at dusk. I hesitate before opening the door; and the door is opened for me. It was Him standing there. I hear a noise, and see in the light of the candle two mice disappearing through a hole in the stone wall.

I cannot see his face clearly because the candle is behind him.

His voice declares: 'Come to me all of you who are tired from carrying heavy loads, and I will give you rest.

'Take my yoke and put it on you, and learn from me, because I am gentle and humble in spirit; and you will find rest. For the yoke I will give you is easy, and the load I will put on you is light.'[6]

I am afraid to enter. I fear the Devil, I fear the Accuser, I fear the Christ, I fear myself.

CHAPTER 17

ECCE HOMO

10 December (Saturday)

I do not intend to look on his face again. I would prefer to think of the wise men of humanity. The Master of the Knowledgeable Ones came past, the incomparable analyst, the matchless disciplinarian. Is not this one master of himself and lord of nature? And here is his friend from the Far East, the politician and counsellor, and his order for everything and everything in its order. I am amazed by them. The Ecce Homo comes to my lips.

There is the Tearful Philosopher and the Laughing Philosopher and the spirits which gather around them. Those over there gyrate in a whirlpool trying to keep their human dignity and self-respect. These over here smell and taste and sense and respect the dust as material which outlives every breath. And the hosts of each party are like stars in the heavens. Ecce Homo. Existentialists or Realists, I am prepared to join with one or the other.

Heraclitus, Pythagoras, Gottama Buddha and the Druids: my soul dances between fantasy and pandemonium. Epicurus, Koheleth, Omar Khayyam, Dafydd ap Gwilym, Baudelaire: I am lost among the gardens and glades and hotels. Lao-tse, Plato, Erigena, Morgan Llwyd, Ann Griffiths: my heart struggles from star to star. Ecce Homo. Within me are heaven and earth and the wheel that never tires.

Zarathustra, Amos and Muhammad: the universe is split. Akenhaton, Hosea, Dante: creation is made whole. Ecce Homo. And my mind is purified by terror and pity.[1]

Jesus of Nazareth, the strange rabbi, the great martyr. Lift the stone, split the wood.[2] Ecce Homo. Come to me, beloved, with your scar and smile.

11 December (The Lord's Day)

In the morning I preached about the true Greatness of the Anointed Servant. My soul trembled throughout the day.

The snow storm blew without mercy and my attempt to return home tonight was fruitless. I succeeded in reaching the centre near by, but there was no possibility of travelling further and I had to return to the haven of my lodging, and I walked for two miles through the snow and ice before I had a lift in a car.

Following the experience, I feel most insignificant, and sick with failure. I am a weak insect, one of myriads of winged creatures and reptiles and caterpillars, and I squeak like a mouse when I hear Time's warriors trampling and squashing above my head. And I boast of being like God and Maker and Saviour!

It is a sweet pleasure to warm in the bed on such a frosty and shivering night, and I must be grateful for being endowed so abundantly with a faculty for warming myself. But it is a gift not an attribute. It is not in my own strength that I can manage as much as this.

Oh God, the Great Giver, forgive me. Overthrow the Huge Idol that fills the temple of my life. Break me into fragments. Fill the temple and dwell in it for ever.

12 December (Monday)

I took the train to escape from the prison of the snow.

But there is no escape from the prison of my life.

*

I wonder if there is salvation in the cell of the hermit?

*

I walked hurriedly into the centre of the happy room and turned and looked quizzically at the face of the Resident. He was standing in the door frame. He had my face. I suddenly realized that it was not a door but a mirror. I was looking at my own picture, and the man in the mirror was imitating all my gestures. I knew that he was my enemy. A well of fury rose from my depths and I took a few threatening steps towards him. He also approached me menacingly.

Our two faces were very close to each other. With my bleary eyes I could see that a certain dullness had come over his eyes. His face was mangled by an ugly smirk. He began moaning and shaking. I saw the spittle accumulating. I was suddenly frightened by his affliction and his depravity.

'You were once an example of perfection. How wise and handsome you were... I put a terrifying angel here to guard you... your conduct was perfect from the day you were created until you began to do evil... You were proud of being handsome and your fame made you act like a fool...'[3]

*

'Lucifer, bright morning star, you have fallen from heaven! In the past you have conquered nations, but now you have been thrown to the ground. You were determined to climb up to heaven and to place your throne above the highest stars. You thought you would sit like a king on that mountain in the north where the gods assemble. You said you would climb to the top of the clouds and be like the Almighty. But instead, you have been brought down to the deepest part of the world of the dead.'[4]

*

After I sat down and became calm I understood that I'd had a waking nightmare.

13 December (Tuesday)

'Lord, the only begotten Son Jesus Christ, Lord God, Lamb of God, Son of the Father, who blots out the sins of the world, have mercy on us. You, who blot out the sins of the world, have mercy on us. You who blot out the sins of the world, accept our prayer. You who sit on the right hand of God, have mercy on us.

'For you alone are holy. You alone are Lord, you alone, Christ, with the Holy Spirit, are the highest in the glory of God the Father.'[5]

14 December (Wednesday)

I praise the notable ones of the earth, kings and princes of the race, those who created and fashioned, those who searched the truth and those who revealed beauty and those who stunned the world with their goodness, those through whom shone the light of the Pure and Holy.

Are these among the princes and kings who greeted Lucifer in the land of the dead saying, 'Now you are as weak as we are! You are one of us! You used to be honoured with the music of harps, but now here you are in the world of the dead. You lie on a bed of maggots and are covered with a blanket of worms.'[6]

Oh Lord of All Grandeur, save *your saints.*

15 December (Thursday)

I went on a journey to address a society consisting of friends of Wales and the Welsh language on the subject of Christianity in Wales today. A generous spirit of common understanding was shown. The challenge is to present the common understanding in collaborative action. But I feel much more confident following the discussion and the conversation with friends.

16 December (Friday)

This is the end of term. The sweet cares of the days before Christmas have commenced already.

The blessed repugnance of the Incarnation has come to astound me once more: the Eternal Word like lightning falling from heaven – willingly and not from his displeasure.

17 December (Saturday)

I feel as if I have been an observer of my own fall.

There are two falls: the Fall from Grace and the Fall from Life. There are two deaths: the Death of the Body and the Death of the Soul. The Second Fall and the Second Death are one; and the other name for both is the Sin against the Holy Spirit.

I saw, by means of the sensual imagination, the Second Fall and the Second Death overtaking me. I saw myself among the scourings of the glorious earth. I know what it is to fade, to wither, to rot, to feed the worm, to subside into stench and dirt.

Oh to be able to breathe, to leap, to live!

Author of Life, come to me, the Great Resurrection, shine on me.

CHAPTER 18

THE SON

18 December (The Lord's Day)

This morning I told the children the story of the Three Kings of Cologne, and I preached about the Wise Men and the Shepherds and, in the evening, about the meaning of the Incarnation.

It is all a blow to my pride, and I was ashamed before God and man. But with the shame, there came a new, exciting, experience which gave a lustre to my discourse in the morning and some confident certainty to my message in the evening.

I don't know how to explain the experience: a sense of the wholeness of the universe.

From time to time previously I have been conscious of the Presence as I preach, but until now the ever-present ego has been gesticulating before Him. But today, somehow, the Word prevailed. The pulpit was a manger, a workshop, a temple, an upper room, and a throne. I saw the shepherds, the common folk and the workers: 'The people who walked in darkness saw a great light. They lived in a land of shadows but now a great light is shining on them.'[1] I followed the pilgrimage of the wise men, the heroes and rulers of mankind, the seekers and the creators and aristocrats: 'Nations will be drawn to your light, and kings to the dawning of your new day.'[2] I was astonished by the unearthly light which shone through the curdling of the ancient seas and the skeins of the distant void. I perceived the unity of the great multitude, and I knew that the many were one in the Sacrifice. And it was a pleasure to recognize myself as a spot of dust in the smoke which arose from the altar of creation.

That is salvation: everyone sitting in his place with Abraham and Isaac and Jacob at the great feast; everyone going to the place prepared for him; everyone seeing that he is part of the pattern of the Design, and that the pattern of the Design is part of him. I am glad of the divine arithmetic: not only is the fraction in the whole but the whole is in the fraction. Thanks for the physiology and astronomy of the Almighty: the Sun from which every sun sprang from shines completely in the most flighty electron that was ever theorized about. Thanks for the Christology of Christ.

'I have been put to death with Christ on his cross, so that it is no longer I who live, but it is Christ who lives in me.'[3]

'How can the teachers of the Law say that the Messiah will be the descendant of David?'[4]

19 December (Monday)

Now the family is in the midst of all the fun and fuss of the Christmas preparations.

The observance of the Advent this year was very scrappy in our family. But from time to time we sang carols around the four candles of the *Adventskranz*.[5] The inquisitiveness and enthusiasm of McTavish are growing, and even dreamy Flanagan is showing signs of eagerness. Ap Siencyn is beginning to theologize about the mysteries of Santa Claus, but his meditation is quiet.

Cards, gifts, recalling ages, changing minds, comparing lists, exchanging books, vowing to start earlier next year – we are in the midst of the trouble.

Christmas is the sacrament of living together and sharing for shepherd and king, the miracle of seeking and receiving together.

The children miss Rhiwallon who is now at his home. But he'll come back.

20 December (Tuesday)

Tonight I looked at the children asleep in their beds; the annoying, dear trinity. And then in my meditation I ventured not to the cell of the hermit but to the stable of the Child.

All the species were there and all the constellations: the fish and the ram, Caer Gwydion and Caer Arianrhod.[6] The shepherds and wise men knelt around it, and quarrymen and coal miners and farmers from Wales, and Virgil and Raphael and Mahatma Gandhi.[7] I saw the horns amidst the shadows, and a fly stood on the Child's nose: a tribute from Beelzebub to his better.

21 December (Wednesday)

I am not going to tell God that I am a fly. The true humility is to acknowledge God in the completeness of all he has done, and to acknowledge ourselves as beings who have been privileged by Him with life and knowing and conscience, vessels of honour and dishonour, wrath and mercy, until we meet in the unity of faith and the knowledge of the Son of God.

22 December (Thursday)

Jesus of Nazareth has common names and titles Christ, Son of God, Son of Man. They are names for the People of God. These names were not given him to shut us out, but to gather us in.

Our Father. Now for the first time I am learning to pray these words. It is said that the word 'our' was not before 'Father' in the original form of the incomparable prayer; and I heard a theologian claiming that Jesus had said 'My Father' and 'Your Father' often, but that there is no mention of him saying 'Our Father' and thereby acknowledging himself a brother to the human family and the divine family. But my soul completely rejects the argument. Did not Jesus pray with his disciples and did he not call with them on the Father who made us all brothers and sisters to himself and to each other?

Our Father, who art in heaven. Hallowed be Thy Name. Thy
Kingdom come. Thy Will be done.
  Abba Father.

I have no words of my own to pray today. 'The Spirit makes
you God's children, and by the Spirit's power we cry out to God
"Father! my Father!"'[8]

'In the same way the Spirit also comes to help us, weak as
we are. For we do not know how we ought to pray; the Spirit
himself pleads with God for us in groans that words cannot
express.'[9]

23 December (Friday)

I saw Mary's tears.
  'Our Mother who art on earth.'

24 December (Saturday, and Christmas Eve, and McTavish's birthday)

A day fit for a king, like some of the days that are past and some
of the days which are to come; and thanks are due to the King
for sharing his royal privileges for one day with McTavish.

The Christmas tree is small but comely. With more fuss than
usual I succeeded in lifting and decorating it, and it seems quite
pretty. Apart from the tree and the odd sprig of mistletoe and
holly and fir, there is little decoration of our rooms this year.
McTavish has lost interest in the coloured paper and Flanagan
is totally unconcerned; and Ap Sienceyn would rather play
with a paper bell than leave it alone.

McTavish enjoys his presents, but his birthday is a foretaste
of Christmas for him. We remember the day of his birth. The
day before Christmas that year was a Sunday, and in the church
where I used to minister a communion service was held at
eight o'clock in the morning, a few hours after the birth of my
first born. It was inevitable that I began the service by saying,
'A child is born to us! A son is given to us!'

The Lively Boy, a red bag on his mother's lap, and his voice like the trumpet of prophecy, and his hands bearing the blessing of the God above the gods, and his weakness and invincible conquest flowing over the heart and over the world!

*

But there. The stockings must be filled. McTavish and Flanagan do not at all believe in Santa Claus – unless they still have a vague idea of him as a little symbolic being halfway between their father and their Heavenly Father. But nothing can shake their faith in the stockings.

25 December (the Lord's Day and the Day of His Birth)

A bag of crimson flesh on Mary's lap and a bag of crimson flesh suspended between the thieves; the helpless bowels of the new born baby and the helpless bowels of the Son of God on the Cross; the cry from the stable and the cry from Calvary; the tears of Mary as she bound him in swaddling clothes and the tears of Mary when she watched others bind his body in cloths; the placing in the manger and the placing in the grave; the shepherds smiling on him and the fishermen rejoicing in the exultation of the resurrection; the wise men giving presents to the small new life and all the wisdom of the world kneeling before the New Man in Christ Jesus –

> *Oh the Breath of the Nostrils of the Son of God, breathe on me. Give me the strength of His Love and the pride of His Effort and His Sacrifice. Fill my soul and body with the passion of the Cross and the pains of the Birth and the victory of the Sacrifice and the astonishment of the Rising from the Dead. Breathe on me, Breath of Life, now and for ever.*

*

Christmas was truly happy. Here are the children emptying their stockings and loading their treasures on our bed. It was easy to take them to the morning service since a kind friend had given them gloves with funny faces on them. The preacher's message was gripping: the promise in every life. And there is a substantial present for each of the children on their return home, and a tasty and moderate dinner for everyone. We had some cooperation and play between lunch and tea and then we removed to the sitting room to sing carols in front of the Christmas tree and to give presents to the whole family. We had to open the parcels from München afterwards before I departed for the evening service, leaving Anna and Taranwen to bring order out of chaos and escort the children to their beds. May the whole world become a home for the family of God the Father and God the Mother.

26 December (Monday)

There are blessings in the hymns and carols of Christmas. 'Adeste fideles' and 'Quem pastores'; 'Hark the Herald Angels Sing' and 'Silent Night'; 'Wele gwawriodd'[10] and 'Wele cawsom';[11] and many from every country, binding earth to heaven, and the pagan to the saint and the home to the White Throne. I particularly like 'Pob seraff, pob sant', a hymn which carries the spirit of a carol. The Easter carols and hymns ought to be richer than the Christmas ones, but they are not. I have felt many times that they ought to exalt Easter rather than Christmas, but on second thoughts all the festivals are one, as long as we greet Christ in all of them. Christmas comes in mid-winter when we need the sun more than ever and when life begins to strengthen. I feel sorry for the Christians of the Antipodes who have to hang on the earth with their heads down and celebrate Christmas in the middle of summer!

27 December (Tuesday)

If McTavish had been born a girl, her name would have been 'Monica Mary'. If Ap Siencyn had been born a girl, her name would have been 'Enid Katrinachen'. In what heaven are these little beings, I wonder? They come out to sing with the heavenly host every Christmas now.

Perhaps that 'Carys Iohanna' or 'Miriam Siân' will come to cheer some Christmas in the future.

28 December (Wednesday)

I went to the Hermit's door once more, and I heard the Voice.

'Come to me, all of you who are tired carrying heavy loads, and I will give you rest. Take my yoke and put it on you, and learn from me, because I am gentle and humble in spirit; and you will find rest. For the yoke I will give you is easy, and the load I will put on you is light.'[12]

I saw him in the light of the candles: the Son of the Carpenter, the Son of Man, the Son of God, the Son of Prophecy. I saw the smile and the scar and the ardent gentleness and the incomparable welcome. The eyes, the nostrils, the hair, the lips – how can I describe the glory of his face? The shoulders, the arms, the hands, and the breath of His closeness – how can I describe the magnificence of His presence? The brightness of the half-light was more than I could bear. I fell down before him and I lay with my face in my hands, and my body shook with contrite repentance and insatiable passion.

There came the touch and the greeting and the command.

'Peace be with you.'

'Mortal man, stand up. I want to talk to you.'

I stood up, and my cell was as before, and the books on the shelves and the papers on the desk, and Christmas gifts on every hand, cards and strings and wrapping paper. But the walls were not frowning on me nor were the cupboards threatening to fall on me. There was a soft and gentle lightness in everything, and a warmth in my breast.

29 December (Thursday)

'My Father has given me all things. No one knows the Son except the Father, and no one knows the Father except the Son and those to whom the Son chooses to reveal him.'[13]

I have been walking the road of acknowledgement:

acknowledging fault and failure and corruption and self-worship. Now, I must tread the path of knowing: God knowing me and me knowing God: knowing Christ and Nature, the Spirit and the Saints, and the soul growing in the All-in-All.

30 December (Friday)

I had better end the diary as the year ends. I have arrived at a turn in the road. Perhaps, when I have matured in my knowledge, another diary would be beneficial for me and the occasional fellow pilgrim.

*

Immanuel: God is with us.

31 December (Saturday)

I travelled to keep an appointment and to spend the night at the home of old friends. We had a late night of talk and laughter and the sharing of memories and amusing complaints and mischievous remarks. They have a greater talent than me with these matters, but I enjoyed all of it. The new year is now knocking at my back as I push myself between the sheets of the bed.

> Oh Accuser and Judge and Gentle Executioner, take me, bare me, scourge me. Crown me with your thorns, nail me on Your Cross, bury me in Your Grave. Free me in your Resurrection. Send me to your people. Keep me in your Grace. For Your Name's sake. Amen.

*

Immanuel: God with us.

NOTES

Introduction

1   John Rowlands, 'Y Llenor Enigmatig,' in *Cyfrol Deyrnged Pennar* (Swansea, 1981), p.23.

2   Pennar Davies, 'Yr Absen Ddwyfol,' in *Y Brenin Alltud* (Llandybie, 1974).

3   R Tudur Jones, introduction in *Cudd fy Meiau* (2nd ed., Swansea, 1998), p.24.

4   Geoffrey F Nuttall, 'Pennar Davies *complexio oppositorum*,' *Journal of the United Reformed Church Historical Society* (12 November–29 December 1996), p.575.

Chapter 1: The Beginning of the Year

1   Brother Lawrence (Nicolas Herman; *c.*1605–91) was accepted to the Carmelite abbey in Paris in 1649 where he became responsible for work in the kitchen – work which he despised but work that he attempted to undertake joyfully and from love of God. He pleads for the practice of the presence of God through prayer and meditation using the intelligence and the imagination. It is evident that he was a considerable influence on Pennar as is seen in *Diary of a Soul* on 16 February and other places, where he also tried to strengthen his devotion by imagining Jesus Christ's face and body.

It is worth noting that the title Pennar chose for his volume *Cudd Fy Meiau*, literally means 'cover my faults', and is a quotation of a well-known Welsh hymn by William Williams, Pantycelyn (see note 4, chapter 4), which in turn reflects the wording of Psalm 19:12. He originally favoured *Dyddlyfr Enaid* [Diary of a soul], a title which I've adopted for this publication.

2   Isaiah 6.5.

Chapter 2: The Accuser

1   Genesis 32.26.

2   1 Corinthians 11.28.

3   Matthew 6.33.

4   Isaiah 6.8.

5   John 12.32.

6   Romans 11.26.

7   2 Corinthians 2.16.

8   John 5.17.

Chapter 3: The Worker and Paterfamilias

1   Psalms 8.

2   Matthew 3.9.

3   This is the poetic name of the Rev. William Rees (1802–83), a leading radical, newspaper editor, poet and noted Independent preacher.

4   This is a couplet from one of David Charles' best-known hymns (1762–1834). He was one of the foremost Calvinistic Methodists of his day.

5   A couplet by R Williams Parry (1884–1956), a leading Welsh poet in the strict metres and in free verse.

Chapter 4: Freedom and Dedication

1   *Imitatio Christi* was the title of the well-known book attributed to Thomas á Kempis (*c.*1380–1471). It provides guidance on following Christ by imitating him. It has been translated into Welsh and the numerous editions in the eighteenth century confirm its popularity.

2   Evan Rees (1850–1923) was highly acclaimed as a preacher, poet and popular lecturer. He officiated at *eisteddfodau* as Archdruid and was widely travelled. He won many poetry prizes, but this poem, 'Jesus of Nazareth', written in strict metres, won him the chair at the World Fair Eisteddfod held in Chicago in 1893.

3   Matthew 20.22.

4   The whole hymn, of which this is the opening couplet, is a striking expression of the hymn writer's desire for Jesus to speak to him despite his doubts. The author is William Williams (1717–91), a prolific author and hymn-writer of the Methodist Revival in Wales. He published about ninety

books and booklets during his lifetime. He wrote both prose and poetry on the soul's journey towards redemption and gave profound practical and spiritual advice to converts who flocked to the religious societies established across the country by the Methodists. He has been described as 'the earliest exponent of Romanticism in European literature' (see entry in Meic Stephens, ed., *The New Companion to the Literature of Wales* (Cardiff, 1998)).

Pennar Davies would have warmed to his emphasis on the place of experience in religion. An excellent English introduction to his work is provided by Glyn Tegai Hughes, *Williams Pantycelyn*, Writers of Wales (Cardiff, 1983).

5 Mark 9.19.

6 2 Corinthians 3.17.

7 Galatians 5.1.

8 James 1.25.

9 Romans 8.21.

10 Ellis Wynne (1671–1734) was a prose writer of considerable acumen and author of an important satirical work, *Gweledigaetheu y Bardd Cwsg*, which proved immensely popular. The reference here is to the work of Jeremy Taylor, which he translated with considerable finesse.

11 Professor W J Gruffydd (1881–1954) was a leading figure in the literary and political life of Wales in the twentieth century. He served as a member of parliament from 1943 until 1950. He edited *Y Llenor*, a quarterly literary magazine, from 1922 to 1951. He was also a scholar and poet of stature.

12 Matthew 12.50.

13 Philippians 2.5.

14 Matthew 4.3.

15 Matthew 4.4.

16 Romans 8.26.

17 Stephen Owen Davies was Labour MP for Merthyr Tydfil from 1934 to 1972. He had some sympathy for the movement for a provincial parliament for Wales and he (together with Cledwyn Hughes, the Member for Anglesey) introduced a bill to that end. But it was thwarted and this left many patriots, including Pennar, bitterly disappointed.

18 The 'Desert Song' (1926) was a popular operetta by Sigmund Romberg, set in the Sahara!

19   Matthew 4.4.

20   Luke 11.42.

21   Matthew 23.23.

22   John 3.8.

23   2 Corinthians 3.17.

24   Galatians 5.1.

25   The Vulgate translation of 1 Corinthians 1.20:'Where is the wise man? ...
       God has shown that this world's wisdom is foolishness!'

26   Cynan was the bardic name of Albert Jones Evans (1895–1970). He
       was a dramatist, poet, lecturer and an important figure at the National
       Eisteddfod.

27   'God is our strength and defence' (tr. Alan Gaunt).

28   'Out of the depths I have cried to Thee'.

29   'O sacred heart, sore wounded' This hymn is a translation by Paul Gerhardt
       (1607–76) from Bernard of Clairvaux, 'Salve mundi salutare' – a lengthy
       hymn in seven sections which concentrate on various members of Christ's
       body. It is not difficult to see why this would have appealed to Pennar given
       his serious attempts to visualize the Master. An English translation has
       been provided by J W Alexander (1804–59).

30   'If God is with me, I shall walk'.

31   'Go out, my heart and seek delight' (trans. Catherine Winkworth and G R
       Woodward).

32   Gerhardt was a Lutheran minister and second only to Luther as a hymn-
       writer. He was an uncompromising Lutheran but he was influenced by
       Roman Catholic mysticism. This would have appealed to Pennar.

33   'To work is to pray'.

34   The Gorsedd was an assembly of bards instituted by the eccentric genius
       Edward Williams (1747–1826) which evolved to be a representative body of
       Welsh life. Among other things, it is responsible for the ceremonies of the
       National Eisteddfod an annual festival held alternately in north and south
       Wales. Pennar quotes here from what seems to be an ancient and lovely
       prayer used at every such eisteddfod.

Chapter 5: Flesh and Spirit

1   'The lusts of the flesh'.

2   There were three Pelagias in the early history of the Church. The second is the one mentioned here. She was an actress in Antioch who was converted under the influence of Saint Nonnus, the bishop of Edessa, and who travelled to Jerusalem wearing a man's clothes. She dwelled there in a cave on the Mount of Olives practising a strict asceticism. She became confused with the first Pelagia, who was a fifteen-year-old girl from Antioch who jumped into the sea around AD 311 to preserve her virginity when soldiers threatened her.

3   John 1.14.

4   For the monks who practised extreme asceticism in Syria and Egypt see H Chadwick, *The Early Church* (London, 1967), and the article on Simon Stylites in the *Oxford Dictionary of the Christian Church*. He is reported to have spent his life on the top of a pillar or column in order to be detached from the world.

5   This is another verse of the hymn by David Charles (see note 4, chapter 3).

6   'Destructive inheritance'.

7   Genesis 1.27–8.

8   An *awdl* is a long poem which employs one or more of the traditional metres which are twenty-four in number. It must be composed in *cynghanedd*, which means that every line must be expressed according to one of four patterns of rhymes and consonants. It is one of the hallmarks of Welsh poetry extending from the sixth century to modern times. It is still one of the major competitions at the National Eisteddfod and the winning bard is rewarded with the Chair at a central ceremony.

9   This is the nom de plume that Pennar chose when writing his weekly diary.

10   Matthew 27.40.

11   Mark 15.30.

12   John 17.21.

13   Luke 4.6–7.

14   Luke 4.8.

15   This was a Welsh-language hymn book in booklet form issued to troops during the Second World War by The New Wales Union which played an

important role in defending certain Welsh interests during and after the war years.

[16]   The author is William Ambrose (1813–73).

Chapter 6: Death and Resurrection

[1]   Matthew 27.46.

[2]   Mark 15.30–31; Luke 23.39; Luke 23.37.

[3]   The phrase is found in the Latin version of the Apostles Creed (before AD 341): 'sub Pontio Pilato crucifixus, et sepultus' – 'who was crucified under Pontius Pilate and was buried'. The reference to Karl Barth is in *Credo* (1935). The same point is discussed in *Dogmatics* (SCM, 1949), 117–18.

[4]   Ann Griffiths (1776–1805) was an exceptional hymn-writer but her stature is based on only thirty-four hymns and a few letters. She was a powerful biblical, dramatic, and theological – yet highly personal – writer. She has gained acceptance in international circles and an English appreciation has been written by A M Allchin in the Writers of Wales series (1976).

[5]   Genesis 1.3.

[6]   John 12.24.

[7]   1 Corinthians 15.36–9.

[8]   1 Corinthians 15.42–3.

[9]   This is a couplet from a hymn by an Independent minister who came under the powerful influences of the Methodist Revival in Wales. His name is John Thomas (1730–1804) and he was a native of Radnorshire.

[10]   This truly wonderful hymn is by Edward Jones (1761–1836). He was a popular poet and satirist.

[11]   *Diwinyddiaeth* [Theology] – a long-established journal discussing theological and allied matters. J D Vernon Lewis (1879–1970) was an outstanding Hebrew scholar who also introduced Karl Barth and his theology to Welsh-language readers at a very early date – certainly prior to 1935. He was principal of the Memorial College prior to Pennar's appointment on his retirement.

[12]   This was the denominational hymn book of the Independents (*Yr Annibynwyr*) at the time.

[13]   These are the first lines of Pennar's favourite hymns by this author. The

translations are somewhat literal. I have not attempted to emulate their poetic qualities in English – for Welsh ears they resonate with meanings which incorporate the whole hymn which they represent.

14   Another segment from one of William Williams' well-known hymns.

15   Dafydd William (1720–94) is the author of a number of hymns which are still popular for their limpid style and religious exuberance. The other hymn writers listed are all noteworthy exponents of their craft.

16   These four lines are part of a magnificent hymn by Ann Griffiths.

17   This is Wales's biggest cultural event when competitions in music, drama, poetry, literature and art are held on the first full week of August. There are numerous attendant activities, events and concerts.

18   1 Kings 10.7 – the Queen of Sheba's words expressing her surprise at Solomon's wealth.

19   Chris Rees was given a twelve-month prison sentence for refusing to obey the Conscription Act and join the armed forces. Directly after the verdict was passed he fought an election for Plaid Cymru in Gower from prison. He was released in August.

Chapter 7: Confession

1   James 5.16.

2   Pennar chose the first three words of this hymn as a title for the first edition – although he did originally favour the title of 'The Diary of a Soul'. The words of the hymn writer echo the words of Psalm 19.12: 'Deliver me, Lord, from hidden faults.'

3   Psalm 90.8.

4   E Tegla Davies (1880–1967) was a major figure on the Welsh literary scene; his forte was satire although he also excelled at writing books for children. He wrote one significant novel, *Gŵr Pen y Bryn*, which was translated into English, and was described by one commentator as 'a significant milestone in the development of the Welsh novel'. Pennar was attracted by his work and provided an appreciation in the Writers of Wales series in 1983.

5   Luke 8.30.

6   Romans 7.24.

7   Leopold von Sacher-Masoch (1835–95) gave us the word 'masochist'. The Marquis de Sade likewise gave us the word 'sadistic'.

8   This refers to the account of the woman caught in adultery in John 8.1–11.

9   T Gwynn Jones (1871–1949) was a scholar and poet of great distinction. He was also a novelist and biographer and he translated a number of classics from English, German and other European languages.

10   He created wild words in my breast
     And drew me avidly to every beautiful picture;
     This is how I move from lust to taste,
     And in the tasting, to long for the lust.

11   This the first line of another hymn by Ann Griffiths based on imagery from Revelation 22.

12   The Independent/Congregational churches of Wales – about 450 in number – meet annually to discuss matters of mutual concern. National and international church affairs and also social and political questions are discussed. It is served by a full time secretary who acts on behalf of the churches in a wide-ranging role. This is the *Undeb* – or Union of Welsh Independents.

13   These are the first words on the title page of one of the earliest books to be printed in Welsh, probably in 1547, by Sir John Prys (1502–55), a native of Breconshire and one of Thomas Cromwell's agents in the dissolution of the monasteries. *Yn y llyvyr hwnn* means 'In this book'.

Chapter 8: Avarice

1   Iolo Goch (*c.*1320–*c.*1398) was an accomplished and wide-ranging poet in the strict metres. He was one of the first to write poems of praise to the gentry and royalty of the period in a particular metrical form known as the *cywydd*.

2   Ben Davies (1840–1930), a renowned preacher and author noted for the clarity of his thought and practical wisdom. He was president of the *Undeb* in 1901.

3   A poet of the Marches (*c.*1400–45) who satirized many of the sins of his day.

4   C C Martindale, *The Message of Fatima* (London, 1950).

5   This is the first line of a hymn by H Elvet Lewis (1861–1953). The last four lines could be translated as 'If God desires my soul/ My soul desires God:/ Oh such love without beginning and end/ On such wonderful love I live.'

He was a minister who served a number of English churches but spent a lengthy ministry in the Tabernacle Welsh Independent Church, King's Cross, London from 1904 to 1940. He was a well-known poet and renowned as a hymn writer of great appeal – many of his hymns are still popular.

6   Matthew 6.24, 25.

Chapter 9: Mammon

1   1 Corinthians 15.58–16.1.

2   This is a hymn by another William Williams (1801–76). It gives a striking account of the story of the Atonement and of the joy which this provides for the believer.

3   John Morris-Jones (1864–1929) was an eminent scholar of great erudition who among other things standardized Welsh grammar. He was a professor at University College, Bangor and raised the literary standards of his day in his lectures, in articles and on public platforms. He introduced a new vein of poetry and 'Psalm to Mammon' satirised the social standards of his day.

4   This is one of the funds established by the *Undeb* for the support of ministers.

5   Matthew 22.21.

6   Matthew 6.19, 21.

7   Luke 1.53; Luke 4.18; Luke 6.20, 21, 38.

8   Luke 9.58.

9   The author of this hymn was Ben Davies (1864–1937). He was a representative of the 'new poetry' in Welsh and won a number of major prizes at the National Eisteddfod. He became president of the *Undeb* in 1926.

10   Luke 18.29–30.

Chapter 10: On a Journey

1   The Remonstrant Church of the Netherlands arranged a theological conference under the aegis of the International Congregational Fellowship at Le-Chambon-sur-Lignon in southern France. The secretary of the *Undeb*, the Rev. E Curig Davies, and Principal Gwilym Bowyer of the theological college at Bangor were Pennar's companions.

2   The conference was followed by a meeting of the World Council

of Congregational Churches at the Ecumenical Institute in Bossey, Switzerland.

3   'To you be the glory, Oh Resurrected One...'

4   Matthew. 27.46.

5   Joel 2.25, 28.

6   This was a meeting of the prime ministers of France, Britain and Russia, and the president of the USA. They were meeting at the Palais des Nations in Geneva at this time.

7   Ulrich Zwingli (1484–1531) was the pioneer of the Reformation in Zurich and his successor was Johann Heinrich Bullinger (1504–75).

8   Keller (1819–90) was a Swiss poet and short story writer.

9   1 Kings 14.27.

10   John 19.22.

11   T H Parry-Williams (1887–1975) was a gifted essayist and poet who was professor of Welsh at Aberystwyth University College.

12   'Behold the Man.'

13   Ephesians 4.13.

14   'How great are God's riches! How deep are his wisdom and knowledge!' Romans 11.33.

Chapter 11: Tossing and Turning

1   The Fourth Ecumenical Council was held in Chalcedon in Asia Minor in AD 451. Leontius lived in the sixth century. Little is known about him but he was an important theologian and he defended the Chalcedonian 'definition' of the relationship between the human and divine nature in Christ.

2   *amo* = I love; *odi* = I hate.

3   August Strindberg (1849–1912) was a Swedish novelist and playwright noted for his misogyny.

4   David Herbert Lawrence (1885–1930) was an English poet and novelist. His work provoked widespread interest in the 1950s and Pennar held him in high regard.

5   The Urdd is the Welsh League of Youth, a movement for children and young people established in 1922. It publishes a number of magazines, runs two residential centres, and holds an annual national eisteddfod, which attracts thousands of youngsters and their parents, and is credited with being the

largest youth festival in Europe. It is based on the principles of fidelity to Wales, Mankind and Christ.

6   'Athanasius against the world'. Athanasius (*c*.296–377), who was bishop of Alexandria, was attacked and exiled by the followers of Arius (*c*.250–336). During his exile he felt that he stood alone. Hence the saying which has become proverbial.

7   This is a brief reference to an Irish theologian, Iohannes Scotus Ergina (*c*.810–876), who believed in God's immanence in His world. In his important work, *De Divisione Naturae*, he considers four aspects of 'Nature', a word which embraces everything in His system. God is the 'Nature which creates' – *Natura Creatix*. This thinker was of considerable interest to Pennar since he also was aware of the 'Presence' in the natural world around him.

8   W N P Barbellion was the nom de plume of Bruce Frederick Cummings (1889–1919), a diarist and a biologist and the author of *The Journal of a Disappointed Man* (London, 1919).

9   Mark 6.3.

10 Dafydd ap Gwilym (*fl.*1320–70) was possibly 'the greatest Welsh poet of all time' (*The Oxford Companion to the Literature of Wales* (Oxford, 1986)). His love poems are memorable and often amusing, but they also reflect a profound love of nature and especially birds, which are seen as 'Nature's own poets and priests in whose activities he discerns the implicit counterparts of his own, since poet and bird are in unison in singing a paean of praise to God for the marvels of His Creation' (*The Oxford Companion to the Literature of Wales*). Hammurabi was king of Babylon from 1750 BC to about 1708 BC and was noted for his laws. Girolamo Savonarola (1452–98) was a Dominican and prior of San Marco in Florence, as well as a prophet and reformer. Henry Ford (1863–1947) was a car manufacturer and pioneer of mass production.

11 Henri Frederic Amiel (1821–81) was a Swiss philosopher and literary figure, author of *Fragments d'un journal intime* (1883).

12 This is the period of considerable unrest in Cyprus and Morocco – seen by many as the last flailings of Empire, of the French and English version.

13 Luke 22.64; John 18.23.

14 Phyllis is a nom-de-plume.

15 A popular Welsh song which purports to commemorate the Battle of the

Marsh of Rhuddlan on the river Clwyd when Caradog, king of Gwynedd, was killed with all his men by the forces of Offa, the king of Mercia.

Chapter 12: Anger

[1]   The author is S J Griffiths (1850–93). The hymn describes how, by clinging to the rock of ages, in the teeth of storms and disasters, the believer will be safe. Even when the universe collapses the rock will stand, and this will be his constant song of joy.

[2]   This is a well-loved hymn by John Dafydd (1727–83) which talks of the Christian being released from his chains and of all the enemies of the soul being captured.

[3]   Origen (c.185–c.254) was a great biblical scholar of the early Church who believed that at the final restoration all beings would be saved, including the devil. His *De Principiis* is the first great systematic presentation of Christianity. He taught at Alexandria and Caesarea.

[4]   Lycanthropy is the ancient belief reflected in fables that people could be transformed into wolves. This is Pennar's joke since his wife's patronymic was 'Wolff' and the German word for the creature is *Wolf*.

[5]   Matthew 5.22.

[6]   Hosea 2.2–3.

[7]   'Do not touch me.' John 20.17.

[8]   A volume containing most of the literary and poetic winners at the National Eisteddfod with accompanying adjudications. The title means 'compositions and adjudications'.

[9]   John 3.16.

[10]   This is a reference to the Latin couplet by Martial (c.40–c.104). The translation by Thomas Brown (1663–1704) is as follows:

> I do not love thee, Doctor Fell,
> The reason why I cannot tell;
> But this alone I know full well,
> I do not love thee, Dr Fell.

[11]   Four lines of a hymn by J H Hughes (1814–93) of Llaniestyn, Gwynedd.

[12]   Romans 1.18.

[13]   Romans 9.22.

Chapter 13: Jealousy

1   Dorothy Leigh Sayers (1893–1957). This was broadcast as a popular drama series, but the authoress was better known as a writer of detective novels, a genre that Pennar's cultural interests (on his own admission) did not include!

2   'The Way of Purification'.

3   Matthew 9.34.

4   Matthew 12.24, 32.

5   In 1940 an extensive area of land to the north of Brecon was appropriated by the military authorities for artillery training. Two hundred and nineteen individuals from fifty-four farms were evicted with little warning and no alternative accommodation provided for them. Pennar felt strongly about this militarization of Wales and joined frequently in protest with members of the Fellowship of Reconciliation at the site of a defunct chapel within the jurisdiction of the army. The name of the mountain area is Epynt.

6   Matthew 11.28–30.

7   This is a bitter comment on the campaigns of Billy Graham, the American evangelist.

8   Dai Dower was a featherweight Welsh boxer who became champion of the British Commonwealth in 1955. Gilbert Harding (1907–66) was one of the best-known broadcasters of his day.

9   Ezekiel 11.17.

10   This is a reference to the 'sermon class' at the college when the students had to preach in front of their tutors and fellow students and then listen to criticisms of their efforts. (Pennar was always constructive and kind in his comments. Not so, one's fellows, as I can aver!)

11   This is a reference to the ascetic saint of the desert, who spent his life on a pillar. His name was Simon Stylites (390–459).

12   'the common people'.

13   Zarathustra (or Zoroaster c.628–c.551 BC) was a Persian prophet who established a new religion based on dualism, that is, the principle that there is a continuous struggle between the god of light and the god of darkness. Laotze (sixth century BC) was the founder of Taoism. Euripides (c.480–406 BC) was a Greek dramatist. Valerius Catullus (c.82–54 BC) was

a Roman poet. Dante Alighieri (1265–1321), Italian poet. Michelangelo (1475–1564), Italian artist. Morgan Llwyd (1619–59), 'a literary genius of a high order' and a Puritan mystic who had come under the influence of Jacob Boehme, the Lutheran mystic. He published eleven works altogether. Feder Mikhailovich Dostoyevsky (1821–81), Russian novelist. Rabindranath Tagore (1861–1941), Indian philosopher. Walter Savage Landor (1775–1864), English novelist. John Donne (1572–1631), English poet. William Butler Yeats (1865–1939), Irish poet.

[14] The river Tarrell flows from Pen-y-fan in the Brecon Beacons joining the Usk to the west of Brecon.

[15] Matthew 6.2.

[16] Philippians 2.5–11.

[17] The original words are found in a hymn by John Williams (1728–1806) of St Athan in the Vale of Glamorgan.

[18] Thomas Iorwerth Ellis (1899–1970). He was a leading educationist, author, churchman and travel writer. He represented Wales on the *Round Britain Quiz* on the BBC for twenty years! This reference is to a book of essays, *In My Bones*, on contemporary Welsh topics.

[19] Taliesin was one of 'two great and authoritative poets who stood together at the very beginning of the Welsh poetic tradition' i.e. the late sixth century. The later folk tale, probably of the ninth century, concerning him in *Hanes Taliesin* (The history of Taliesin) refers to the intention of Ceridwen, after she had brewed the magic cauldron, to give some of the potion to her son but mistakenly giving it to Gwion Bach (Little Gwion). There follows a chain of incredible events which end with Gwion being adopted and renamed Taliesin. The theme of this myth is that of poetic inspiration.

[20] The closing couplet of another great hymn by David Charles.

[21] This is sometimes credited to Ignatius Loyola (1495–1556) but according to the *New Catholic Encyclopaedia* it was in being years before his time:

> Soul of Christ, sanctify me
> Body of Christ, save me
> Blood of Christ, refresh me
> Water from Christ's side, wash me
> The radiance of Christ's face, illuminate me.

[22] Pennar chose four verses from the oldest version of this Latin hymn found at the Bodleian Library, Oxford, adding the third verse from a later source.

The first line of the original reads 'Jesu, Dulcis memoria'.

Jesus, sweet remembrance,
Granting its heart true joys,
But above honey and all things
Is being in Your sweet presence.

O Jesu! Light of all below!
Thou font of life and fire!
Surpassing all the joys we know,
And all we can desire.

Hail, Thou who man's Redeemer art,
Jesu, the joy of every heart;
Great Maker of the world's wide frame,
And love's purest light.

O sweetest Jesu
When you visit our hearts
You dispel the darkness of the mind
And fill us with sweetness.

O JESUS, king most wonderful!
Thou Conqueror renowned!
Thou Sweetness most ineffable!
In whom all joys are found!

(*This translation was provided by Mr Wyn Thomas of The National Library.*)

23   'O quanta qualia sunt illa Sabbatta...' 'Oh what charm the Sabbaths have...'

This is a hymn by Peter Abelard (1079–1142). The reason for mentioning reconciliation between him and Bernard of Clairvaux is that the latter had been mainly responsible for condemning him for heresy.

Chapter 14: Pride

1   The translator has ventured to offer his own translations of these mediaeval words.

2   The explanations here are in the original mediaeval texts.

3   This couplet comes from a *cywydd* entitled 'The Seven Deadly Sins and the Passion of Christ'. Authorship uncertain.

4   A line from an ode by R Williams Parry.

5   James 1.11.

6   The meaning of 'plutus' is wealth and Pluto was the god of the underworld in Roman mythology.

7   An iconic painting by Sydney Curnow Vosper (1866–1942) of a small Baptist chapel with worshippers in various postures with the figure of Siân Owen, in her magnificent shawl, centre. It is claimed that the devil's face is discernible in the folds of the shawl although Vosper denied that this effect was deliberate.

8   The author of this pithy saying was the poet Ieuan Deulwyn (*fl.c.*1450) but it could have been inspired by a similar thought expressed in Ecclesiastes 3.15: 'Whatever happens or can happen has already happened before.'

9   Ben Bowen (1878–1903) was a promising young poet and man of letters who sadly died at the age of 25. John Gruffydd Hughes (Moelwyn; 1866–1944) was an able scholar and minister. He was known as a promising poet in his youth and two hymns that he wrote are still sung by Welsh congregations.

10   The author of the hymn is Casper Heunisch (1620–90), a Lutheran minister.

> Oh Eternity, you word of thunder,
> Oh sword which pierces the soul.
> Oh Eternity, you word of joy,
> Who revives me more and more.

11   lit. 'seize the day' i.e. enjoy the pleasures of the moment which is what the following quotation from a well-known Welsh poem also states.

12   *Culhwch and Olwen* is one of the earliest Welsh tales dating from *c.*1100.

13   Mark 10.30.

14   Caer Pedryfan is probably a four-turreted fort in the Arthurian land of magic and fairies. Pennar may be placing this in contra-distinction to the formal Christianity of Byzantium while at the same time pleading for their coming together. Does he mean a marriage of creativity and rationality?

15   This is a reference to a strike by the theological students at the Memorial College, Brecon. Following the morning service the president of the Junior Common Room approached Pennar and declared that the students would not be attending lectures nor cooperating in the work of the college until the authorities considered their complaints. 'They were annoyed that there was no room for them in the administration of the institution, that

their views were constantly being disregarded and that they were treated like children and not as adults.' (D Densil Morgan, *Pennar Davies* (Cardiff, 2003)). There was also some disgruntlement about the dispersion of grants and the standard of food had seriously deteriorated. But one of the main complaints was the hierarchical way in which the college was run. The tutors had very little contact with the students and showed little interest in their personal lives.

Despite threats of expulsion, the students withstood the approaches of the staff and even managed to interview the staff singly and mercilessly! By Sunday 20 November, the strike was over and the students felt that changes would be introduced. Densil Morgan makes the comment, 'Whatever were Pennar's gifts, consideration of the minutiae of students' lives was not among them.' Dewi Lloyd Lewis, who was a student at the time, comments, 'I can say quite unequivocally that Pennar Davies' nobility and strength became apparent during those painful and extraordinary days' (quoted in Morgan, *Pennar Davies*). It may well be that Pennar entrusted much of college life to the students themselves and respected them as companions in education – a status they could not fully appreciate. In other words, he thought too highly of their abilities. This partly explains his disappointment and genuine sorrow at the turn of events. Perhaps he was too genial and reserved to be a principal, and theological students are not the easiest to contain!

[16] Malpomene was the Greek muse of tragedy and Thalia the muse of comedy.

[17] Powys (1872–1963) was renowned as a lecturer, especially in the USA, but returned to his Celtic roots in 1934. 'He was a prolific writer in several forms [but] Powys was at his best as an autobiographer and novelist' (*The Oxford Companion to the Literature of Wales*). Huw Menai or Huw Owen Williams (1888–1961) was a political agitator and journalist who published four volumes of poetry and although he was Welsh speaking he composed in English.

[18] Philippians 2.7.

[19] Lleu was the Celtic god of light.

Chapter 15: The Divide

[1] Genesis 3.5.

[2] Matthew 5.13.

[3] John 20.28.

[4] Matthew 4.9–10.

[5] Thermopylae. This is where the Greeks under the command of the king of Sparta withstood, for three days, the Persian army in 480 BC.

Chapter 16: Rats

[1] 'The Great Mother' – the goddess of fertility in the Eastern Roman Empire. Saint Anthony was the founder of hermitical monasticism in the fourth century AD.

[2] Matthew 27.42.

[3] Mark 12.32.

[4] Philippians 2.8–11.

[5] 'The Way of Purification', 'The Way of Enlightenment', 'The Way of Unity'.

[6] Mark 11.28–30.

Chapter 17: Ecce Homo

[1] Some of these names have appeared previously. Heraclitus (c.535–c.475 BC) was a Greek philosopher; Pythagoras (c.563–c.483 BC) was a religious teacher and philosopher; the Buddha (sixth century BC) was the founder of Buddhism; Epicurus (361–270 BC) was a Greek philosopher; Koheleth is the preacher/philosopher whose work is found in the Book of Ecclesiastes in the Old Testament; Omar Khayyam (?1048–?1122) was a Persian poet and mathematician; Charles Baudelaire (1821–69) was a French poet; Achnaton (1379–1362 BC) was the Egyptian king who attempted to establish monotheism; Morgan Llwyd (1619–59) was the author of eleven books (of which three were in English). He was a Puritan but had come under the influence of the Lutheran mystic, Jacob Boehme. He emphasized personal experience rather than orthodox beliefs. Llwyd has been described as a 'literary genius of a high order'.

[2] This is a saying attributed to Jesus in the *Gospel according to Thomas* dating from about AD 140.

[3] Ezekiel 28.12, 14–15, 17.

4   Isaiah 14.12–15.

5   This prayer is found in the book *Allwydd neu Agoriad Paradwys i'r Cymry* (A key or opening to paradise for the Welsh) printed by John Hughes (Hugh Owen; 1615–86) in Liege. He was a Jesuit priest who had a superb grasp of literary Welsh.

6   Isaiah 14.10–11.

Chapter 18: The Son

1   Matthew. 4.16 and Isaiah 9.2.

2   Isaiah 60.3.

3   Galatians 2.19, 20.

4   Mark 12.35.

5   *Adventskranz* i.e. Advent Wreath.

6   Gwydion and Arianrhod are mentioned in the fourth part of the *Mabinogion*, but here they are different names for the Milky Way. *Caer* means fort.

7   Virgil (70–19 BC) was a Roman poet and Raphael (1483–1520) was an Italian painter.

8   Romans 8.15.

9   Romans 8.26.

10 A well-known Welsh carol which talks of the eternal design coming to fruition in Christ.

11 Another well-loved carol composed by Dafydd Jones (1711–77), a drover who also translated many of Isaac Watts' hymns into Welsh.

12 Matthew 11.28–29.

13 Matthew 11.25–26.

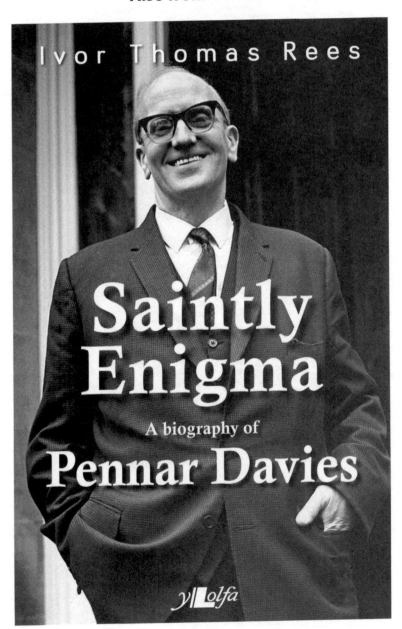

Ivor Thomas Rees

Saintly
Enigma

A biography of

Pennar Davies

Y Lolfa

£9.95

Pointers
to Eternity
Dewi Rees

y Lolfa

£12.95

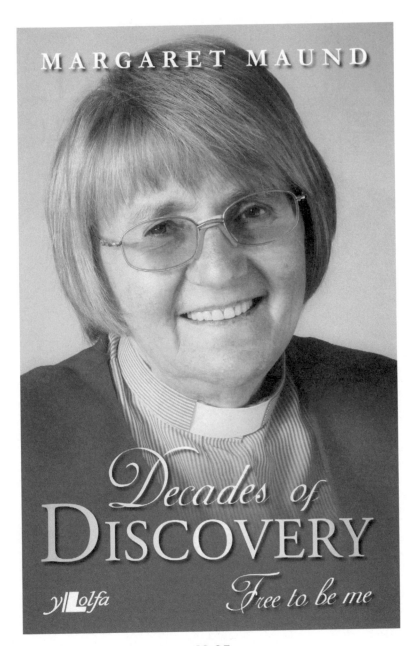

MARGARET MAUND

Decades of
DISCOVERY

y Lolfa

Free to be me

£9.95

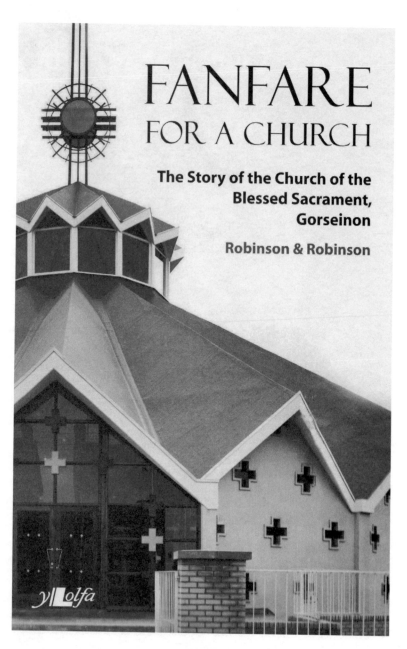

FANFARE
FOR A CHURCH

The Story of the Church of the Blessed Sacrament, Gorseinon

Robinson & Robinson

yLolfa

£6.95

Diary of a Soul is just one of a whole range of publications from Y Lolfa. For a full list of books currently in print, send now for your free copy of our new full-colour catalogue. Or simply surf into our website

www.ylolfa.com

for secure on-line ordering.

TALYBONT CEREDIGION CYMRU SY24 5HE
e-mail ylolfa@ylolfa.com
website www.ylolfa.com
phone (01970) 832 304
fax 832 782